The Therapist's New Clothes

A Memoir

4869 Main Street
P.O. Box 2200
Manchester Center, Vermont 05255
www.northshire.com/printondemand.php

The Therapist's New Clothes

ISBN Number: 978-1-60571-034-1
Library of Congress Number: 2009905785

Names and identifying characteristics of clinicians, colleagues, and clients have all been changed so as to protect privacy. The exceptions are clinicians Sherri and Dr. Cole.

Building Community, One Book at a Time
This book was printed at the Northshire Bookstore, a family-owned, independent bookstore in Manchester Center, Vermont, since 1976. We are committed to excellence in bookselling. The Northshire Bookstore's mission is to serve as a resource for information, ideas, and entertainment while honoring the needs of customers, staff, and community.

Printed in the United States of America
using an Espresso Book Machine from On Demand Books

Also by Judith D. Schwartz

The Mother Puzzle: A New Generation Reckons with Motherhood

Tell Me No Lies: How to Face the Truth and Build a Loving Marriage
(co-authored)

For Tony and Brendan

The Therapist's New Clothes

***

By

Judith D. Schwartz

"We may have thought there was bad stuff in there, but we didn't know how bad. But since it was in the name of healing, we accept it."

D.H. Lawrence

"Psychoanalysis is that mental illness of which it believes itself to be the cure."

Karl Kraus

YEAR ONE

When I met Lucy, my first psychotherapy client, I expected the kind of complaint, syndrome, or pathological personality I had studied at graduate school. Instead, she offered me a metaphor.

It was a cool Saturday morning in September. I was nervous; wouldn't it be obvious to everyone, client and colleague alike, that I felt like a fake? To honor my entry into a new profession I had chosen "a look": I wore sleek black pants and a nifty blue free-flowing jacket, an outfit not too trendy but not untrendy either, with just the hint of an artistic flair. After much deliberation I decided that wearing my hair in a ponytail would differentiate my "therapist" self from my civilian, freelance writer, new mother self. Pulling my hair back bestowed on me a more prudent, not-so-wild attitude, one befitting a mental health professional. I wanted to feel tidy inside too, as though I could hold scattered nerves at bay with an elastic tie.

I rode the El train, lumbering along at a leisurely weekend pace, to the mental health Agency in downtown Chicago. I had my own office for the day, complete with a shelf full of generic mental health books (the PDR, the DSM IV, etc.), a few well-tended flower pots, and a south-facing view that as often as not invited comment from clients as a projection of their mood: "Such a bright, sunny day!" "Oh, it's *gray* again. . ." I had memorized various administrative procedures: which form goes into which file; how to work the phones. I had psyched myself up, assuring myself that by sitting and listening I was unlikely to inflict any lasting psychological harm upon my unsuspecting clients. I did a few yoga stretches. I practiced looking compassionate and wise.

At 10:00 AM sharp the phone rang in my office, jarring me out of a calming mountain pose. Lucy, who I had spoken with only to set up this appointment, had arrived. I stood up, reinserted an errant bobby pin, and strode briskly and evenly down the hall to the waiting room like a runway model showcasing the utmost in sanity.

Lucy was a young woman, two years out of college, with reddish hair shaved nearly to the follicle and bright green eyes that suggested a lively mind. Here was her situation, as gleaned from our conversation and the Agency intake form: she was lost. She had been on an educational conveyer belt, moving from grade to grade as scheduled, and in declining to go to graduate school (law school had been a possibility) she was left without a plan. She lived just miles away from her parents and two older brothers in the suburbs, but avoided seeing them, and her closest friends had left the area. Aside from attending to a dull job that if nothing else would look decent on her resume, she didn't know what to do with herself.

Here was her metaphor: she couldn't keep her Filofax in order. "Look at this," she said to me with exasperation, shuffling through it for effect. "I'm shedding pages as I go. I know that if I could just get my date book and lists in order then everything would be okay." The Filofax was shiny red vinyl. She kept it on her lap, in her hands, as though everything I might need to know about her was contained within.

"I see," I said, as knowingly and sympathetically as I could.

The entire session centered on that motif: the chaos around her that reflected the chaos she was feeling inside. She cited her apartment: "My stuff is such a mess that my roommate wants to partition every room — even the kitchen." Her neighborhood: "As soon as I moved in a few months ago, they started doing construction on the road. The whole sidewalk is torn up so I have to use a back alley and go through the basement." Even her standing vis a vis the U.S. Postal Service: "Somehow my change-of-address card got botched up and all my mail has been going to a postbox all the way across town. I can never get there during business hours. I rushed over yesterday and got there two minutes after they closed."

Lucy didn't smile — it seemed a matter of principle — and she spoke in an ironic deadpan. But a glint in her eyes said that she didn't lack for humor and was at least a little amused by her own fate.

She used this metaphor with exquisite consistency, weaving it in and out of her monologue with the thematic agility of a highly skilled essayist. The notion of disarray came to be a touchstone in our work together; as in our own private code, she would let me know how she was feeling by how neatly she had been able to keep her Filofax. It also came to mirror what I was to go through during my clinical training.

* * *

I believed so wholeheartedly in psychotherapy that I *became* a psychotherapist. I too, for as long as I can remember, felt an internal anarchy. My thoughts and feelings confounded me; they looped back in upon each other, forming a kind of closed circle from which I could not break out. There was never a day when I could say I felt okay. The therapists I had worked with — and there were several, strung along the geographical stopping points of my adult life — seemed so orderly, so sure of the inner logic of life that I trusted they could put me together, reassembling the ill-fitting pieces of my mind. Indeed, for the duration of a session, if I concentrated enough I could be suffused by their reassuring presence and feel okay for a while. With the therapist's help I could style a narrative of my life that made sense — or at least held the promise of making sense.

While the old stereotype of the clinician had been male, cerebral, distant (and often bearded), there was, I came to see, a separate, more contemporary, realm of female therapists. In urban areas and sophisticated suburbs throughout the country, you could find kindly professional women housed in private, tastefully-appointed offices, radiating empathy and generating enough maternal energy to warm the room. These women — and of course they weren't just women, but that was how I perceived it — spoke the language of longing, emptiness, and pain with a lucidity that suggested universal grace. My afflictions no longer felt so lonely.

This was not just the Oedipal game anymore, with analyst and analysand wrestling over resistance and defense. It drew on the heart, not just the head. A new-breed therapist would meet you where your feelings were, sit with you through your pain like a midwife to healing and awareness. The approach, I would later learn, was psychodynamic psychotherapy informed by neo-analytic models like Self Psychology and Object Relations Theory. Such clinical schools emphasized the relationship between therapist and client as the means to growth. In contrast to traditional analysis, however, it was more important for the transference — the shift of feelings toward a parent or other significant person to the clinician — to be *experienced* than interpreted. These ideas were constructs that I would later regard as gospel. As a patient (client) the process touched on something deeper and more raw. I was hooked.

To my mind these lady clinicians, with a youth that belied their apparent wisdom, were the true guardians of the stories of people's lives. They understood their clients as no one else could. Their all-important task was to relieve pain by unlocking memory and revealing the tale within. Only then could remembrances be reworked, recast, and redeemed. Those I consulted assured me that this internal excavation would ease the discomfort that had plagued me all my life. I was sure they knew something I didn't know. It felt so good to be around them that I wanted to *be* one of them.

Why wouldn't I? Here was a field I could go into and do interesting, intellectually-challenging work on a flexible schedule, maybe out of my own home. I could make a contribution to society, easing pain one client at a time. I could draw on traditionally feminine qualities, a penchant for relating and caretaking, in a way that, it seemed to me, was rewarded and valued by society. A therapist was, by definition, an authority and had respect. I certainly seemed to have a knack for being a therapy *patient*, making subtle but illuminating connections between the past and the present; these people apparently liked the way I think. Maybe I could become a therapist. It seemed a natural progression. And maybe, although I never articulated this to myself, if I had access to the secrets of mental health I'd be able to apply them to myself.

As it happened, my professional writing had long taken a psychological slant. Well, say *pop*-psychological. My clip-file was plumping up with pieces like, "The Scales of Passion: When One Loves More"; "When You Out-Earn Your Man"; and "Love, Sex, and the Bottom Line". I even wrote a *Cosmo* quiz, arguably the peak of the genre. I was drawn to psychological topics. I had always been an observer. Along with the awareness that all was not right with myself came an appreciation that other people have secrets and doubts. I knew anxiety well; I found it natural to name and assuage it. I could calm readers down, if not myself. In time my understanding of psychology grew, and with that came a desire to deepen it.

For a long time I toyed with the notion of someday shifting direction and getting an MSW or like degree and testing my own therapeutic skills. "You'd make a wonderful therapist," friends would say. "You're such a good listener." They joked that talking to me was like having psychotherapy by proxy. I did care about what others were feeling and people tended to confide in me. I never felt closer to someone than when we were sharing sadnesses. Getting to that level with someone created an opening in the invisible fence of isolation that otherwise surrounded me. That's how you *really* got to know a person, I believed. No surface, have-a-nice-day stuff for me.

Mostly this was an idle fantasy and I never thought I would act upon it. But then my husband, Tony, and I left New York for Chicago and I felt disconnected from my writing and my writer friends. On slow days I started going to the library at the university where Tony taught to make notes about different masters programs in the city. I attended some informational sessions in downtown Chicago about one school and inquired about part-time status. Then I made an appointment with the admissions liaison from one highly-regarded program and at the end of our meeting she said, "Go take the GREs. Get your application in within a month, and perhaps you could start as early as this fall."

"This fall? Uh, I was just thinking about maybe looking into the options...This fall? Oh, *why not?*"

In truth I had been beginning to feel a bit restless and lost and was looking for a distraction from myself. And what better to get away from myself than to start focusing on *other* people's problems?

I went into gear. I took the GREs, filled out the application, and joined that fall's entering class. I was a dedicated student the whole year, at the end of which my son Brendan was born.

This is the narrative of my career switch that I looked forward to telling:

A young woman struggles for years with sadness, nervousness, and numerous random psychological complaints due to a highly sensitive temperament and certain early childhood experiences. She becomes a journalist. Magazine assignments take her out of herself. Having a mission makes her feel she belongs; her notebook and questions provide a ready link to others. Yet even as her credits and Rolodex grow some absence gnaws at her, like hunger.

Through the most astute psychotherapy and courageous self-reflection she is able to work through difficult feelings and memories and live richly and happily in the present. She meets and marries a lovely man — the son of a journalist — and in time they have a child. She is lonely no more. Her transformation is so successful and so dramatic that she feels compelled to become a therapist herself, plying the magic wand of empathy and understanding in the service of other people's emotional well-being. As the story reaches its denouement Our Heroine stands holding hands with all her previous therapists and, in unison, they take a bow: hard work but well worth it. With her lovely husband and adorable son, this wise and compassionate journalist-turned-therapist lives sagely and blissfully ever after.

Sounds good. However, this story was not to be.

* * *

After the initial jitters subsided I realized I liked doing psychotherapy even more than I expected. Not only that: I was good at it. Bonnie, my supervisor, a warm, effusive woman with several decades of clinical experience and a sense of mission in her work, cooed with delight as I reported from my sessions: "You're gifted! You put your heart and soul into this!" I had three clients, all young women, and I cared about them. I brought that caring into work with me each Saturday. I'm sure they perceived it. I was becoming important to my clients the way my own therapists had become important to me.

The process excited me not only as a long-time client reveling in the privilege of being let in on the trade, but also as a writer. I found clinical work to be a literary experience. For me, practicing psychotherapy proved to be a lot like deep reading. My clients defined themselves through voice and selective detail; I experienced the gradual unfolding of character as each told her story, session by session as in scenes or chapters. As a listener, I would submit to the tale, imagining what the world looked like through the client's eyes. I felt precisely the same absorption as when taken in by a book, the same receptiveness and suspension of my own internal rhythms.

Other clinicians have described this tenor of mental engagement involved in doing therapy. Freud wrote about "evenly suspended attention". More recently, therapist and Buddhist Mark Epstein alluded to "bare attention". Listening at that pitch of concentration does have a meditative quality, which at once broadens and focuses your attunement. It is an exercise in listening to your own inner voice even as you relinquish its hold on you.

Plus, in doing psychotherapy, character in a literary sense loomed large. I was continually struck by the truth of the fiction writers' rule that character determines fate. Things happened to each client that could have happened in just that way *only* to them, events that derived naturally, even inevitably, from their personalities. My clients presented themselves through the fears and failings that preoccupy them. As a result, they come across as vividly exaggerated, almost Dickensian characters. And like Dickens' creations, the more extreme portrayal is ultimately the most true.

I couldn't help but think of Lucy as a kind of latter-day White Rabbit out of *Alice in Wonderland*, running down the street clasping her well-thumbed neon-red Filofax and crying out "I'm late! I'm late! For a very important date!" For every background detail Lucy offered built upon the theme of frantic disorganization. She described, for instance, how her mother used to compulsively copy down recipes and then be unable to find them when she wanted to cook, so they'd end up eating out. (Grilled cheese or chicken tenders, puzzles on the children's menu and a cup of crayon stubs.) Or how, when traveling, she left her passport and credit cards at a hostel, and took two entire days out of her trip to sort it out. The near-exasperating repetition of her reports was what made her so genuine.

Equating clinical work with reading was the precise complement to being a client myself, which I had found much like *writing*. The creative satisfaction I got from the sheer opportunity to exercise my own voice was one of the most compelling aspects of therapy. Now that I was on the other side I could sense the pleasure my clients derived from performing and hearing their own voices performed, from having the chance to emphasize and elaborate on detail in accordance with what they felt, from having an attentive audience. Their enjoyment of this process — the out-loud equivalent of what I did as a writer — pleased me.

Yet more profound was the experience of another person opening herself up to me like a book. The combination of my clients' need and my heightened focus on them created an intimacy that dissolved that stubborn barrier between me and the rest of the world. Despite my love of words I was often too distracted by the static interference of my own mind to read, something that saddened and frustrated me. The intensity of sharing that takes place in therapy recreated the vivid clarity I experienced when a book did manage to reach me or when I reached out to others with my pen.

Marta, my second client, had wavy brown hair worn loose and long. Her soft, delicate features contrasted with the rugged hardware with which she adorned herself: chains, oversized buckles, and as many metal studs as her ears could bear. She experienced every situation as part of a potential or ongoing romance. And romantic encounters *did* seem to happen to her at a pretty impressive rate, romance circa 1990s Chicago with all the newest lingo and hip alternative settings. She was often on the edge of ecstasy or heartbreak. To quote Liz Phair, downtown Chicago's own pop diva, Marta was "exiled in Guyville."

Of my clients, Marta alone had what is known in mental health circles as a "history". In the spring of her freshman year of college in California — she was now finishing school closer to home — she had, as she put it, "crashed." She was put on antidepressants, which she still took under a psychiatrist's supervision. She recalled crying ceaselessly for weeks. There she sat before a droning television as her mother bustled about and offered glib rationales for her daughter's problems ("I never liked that roommate of yours...") Marta's fear of another depression was ever-present; there was always a hint of vulnerability beneath her cheer and metal armor.

My third client was Ellen. A slim African-American woman of about 25, she combed her hair back straight and wore dressy slacks and a blouse (she worked at Marshall Fields, a few blocks away) to most sessions. Talkative and opinionated, she was always on a crusade — against a boss, an insurance company, or a friend. She portrayed herself as perennially misunderstood. She would often begin the session by reporting an incident, usually with someone peripheral to her life, like a salesperson or someone taking pizza orders on the phone, where she was treated rudely or thoughtlessly and was forced to set the record straight. ("So I said to the guy, "I'm *paying* for service and I *expect* service...") I was impressed by how she managed to get into these minor skirmishes in nearly every transaction or exchange.

As the weeks went on and we racked up sessions, I would become familiar with the various characters in each of my client's lives and begin to draw my own conclusions, as in a who-dun-it. Marta, for example, had divorced parents who would each come and go at their will, and an ex-boyfriend she chased after until he turned around and chased her. After one melodramatic phone call from the ex that I was treated to word for word, I jotted down in my notes: "Sam also seems fragile and longing for parental care. Hence the emotional charge and painful ambivalence of their relationship, the desire to merge followed by the fear of engulfment," knowing that I would need more facts and details to have a sense of whether this was true. I would ride that suspense, give hints to the client as to what might be going on beneath the surface, and continue listening, holding all the possibilities in my mind and periodically checking back with them.

As in fiction, sometimes a minor character will make a cameo appearance and spark interest. Once Marta described her great aunt, a newspaper columnist of some local repute in the 40s. "She raised children and she succeeded in a man's job," she said. "Politicians feared her for what she knew. She had as much respect as anyone in town." Because of who she was, not because of any man, I pointed out. I had the image of this relative standing proud in crisp professional attire, her Chanel-type suits contrasting absurdly with Marta's heavy metal and wild, untamed hair. I wanted more of that great aunt. I wanted to expand her role in the narrative. I wanted her to be a motif, her independence and resolve providing a model for Marta to aspire to.

I played with this a bit, concluding the session by alluding to the relative's belief in the curative powers of a finely-pressed outfit. This closed the appointment neatly as it might have ended a short story, and Marta laughed. Although I waited, this woman, and the sartorial irony she represented, never returned.

For two hours each Monday morning I met with Bonnie for supervision. I would ride the El train downtown, ripe with the precious details of my Saturday sessions. I looked forward to putting words to my fleeting intuitions as I lay bare all I had kept in confidence. I was excited to absorb Bonnie's ample knowledge, to better understand the cruel logic of psychic pain. We dissected my process notes the way a scholar examines a text, reading between the lines, extracting themes from the material, enlarging upon the specifics.

Bonnie invariably found nuances that I missed. Didn't I notice that when Ellen came in wearing a nice dress and make-up and said, "Can we turn on the light?" she was telling me: "I want to be seen today" or "I want you to look at me"? And when she later said, "Now that I earn more do I need to pay a higher fee for my sessions?" she was broadcasting the message: "I'm proud of my new earnings."

Every exchange — from the greeting at the door to the transition to a new topic — seemed to burst with significance. The microscopic tendencies of my mind, my too-highly-tuned antennae, worked to my advantage. I would catch the terse evasions or transitory shadows of discomfiting awareness, which rounded out our understanding of each client. In turn, Bonnie would impart to me trade secrets, such as: "When emotions seem to be getting too intense, you can dilute things by making a universal comment, like, "In these kinds of situations *many people feel...*" and instructive gems like: "when someone hasn't received enough maternal affection in childhood they have no stranger anxiety; they'll attach to anyone." I felt the pride of being invited into an elite club. I hung onto her every word.

With Lucy, Bonnie's advice was to "stay within the metaphor." To offer an interpretation now would be too much, like a too-bright light shined in the face. Had I said, "Who are you kidding with this Filofax stuff? It's not going to fix anything. You're confused and you are projecting that all over the place, using the disarray around you to describe what you feel," she would have run screaming out the door. The indirectness of metaphor allowed her to work through her struggles at her own pace.

Hey, I thought, I was born for this. As a writer, I could carry a metaphor. I could use language with precision to test out theories without blowing a client's self-protective cover. I could modulate the tone of a therapeutic dialogue, introducing practicality and levity from time to time as appropriate, so that the material never felt too overwhelming.

And since I had spent my whole life, in therapy and out, battling psychological distress — the internal backdrop to what would seem to anyone a pretty good life — I could pick up on the faintest traces of suffering a client might be feeling. There was no one who would sit in the office with me and feel alone in her pain.

*   *   *

This was a funny time. I was starting a new profession and also embarking on the double life of a working mother. Until the day I met Lucy, I was home full-time with my new baby. I was blessed with a beautiful, bright, little boy who lent reason and rhythm to my days. I was feeding him from my own breast, nurturing him with my love, and he was flourishing.

Embraced in the love of this sparkling tiny child, I was enjoying the greatest contentment I had ever known. If, as I now understand it, I had always experienced the world at an awkward remove, as if behind glass, my son provided a new meeting point. With this child I had a link to others as never before. Every new baby is a conversation piece and Brendan was a head-turner even then. I had the blithe charisma of the proud new mother. People talked to me, told stories I only now had a framework for.

Frankly, the suburb we lived in had been a bit dull without children or a full-time job, a definite reason graduate school had appealed to me. Suddenly, I appreciated the sedateness and the predictable grid of its streets. I could see that points of attention — playgrounds, community bulletin boards, modest but prospering gardens — appeared at a pace ideally suited to someone navigating a baby stroller. The houses had just enough architectural individuality to sustain visual interest: Tudors and Victorians, the newly-prized classic bungalows. Then there was Lake Michigan, lined with beaches and mansions.

On Saturdays and Mondays I would don my stylishly-artistic professional dress, clip back my hair, and go downtown, immersing myself in the busy world of the Agency. On other days I would leave my hair loose, toss on whatever was cleanest and nearest, and wheel Brendan around the suburban streets. Together we would wander in and out of parks and boutiques and have the kind of casual exchanges that make life in towns like ours pleasant. ("Four months. How old's yours?" "I'm an East Coast transplant too.") I could find a connection — a common friend, interest in a new baby product, shared news about local events — with nearly everyone I met. It was a happy arrangement. We were within walking distance of the university where my husband taught and I was accumulating credits toward my degree. We had a wonderful family life and I had satisfying and engaging new work.

Yet there was an undercurrent of uneasiness. My mood was like a soaring balloon caught in a breeze. It was up there, all right, but felt uncomfortably untethered. I was racing around enough as it was. But then if I wasn't in an actual rush I didn't know how to stop. I started finding myself sleepless for long stretches in the middle of most nights.

"What do you think is going on?" I asked Tony, who is a night owl by nature so that the middle of my night found him still awake with a book. "Do you think I'm *too happy?*"

"I don't know," he said. "Maybe you're just adjusting to your new schedule and all these new things."

So I lay awake, uncomfortably aware that not sleeping was never psychologically a good sign.

At one point Tony went away for a few days on a magazine assignment. It was good money. He was thrilled. I panicked about his leaving, way out of proportion to the situation. I was clearly strung out, so I remembered what every advice book had told me about being a new mother: don't forget to do good things for yourself. Great idea... something nice for myself. I made an appointment for a shiatsu massage and left Brendan with Nina, a writer friend already nostalgic for her sons' babyhoods, while I rushed to the center of town to get the stress wrung out of me.

In a shiatsu massage, the healer moves around with you on a mat, guiding your body into stretches and poses. It's like an intimate, stylized dance. I stretched and twisted and discovered that tension had made its way to places I didn't know tension could reside: in my buttocks, in my toes. The man I worked with, Matt, massaged and pulled my fingers, drawing the tension from them.

Towards the end of the massage Matt paused to offer a diagnostic report. He was a bit younger than me and quite handsome. Hair in a ponytail (his uniform, I supposed), lean and strong. Boy he must get a good workout doing this, I thought.

"I sense a whirlwind," he said solemnly as we sat cross-legged on the mat in our sweats. "Your energy is all over, going in different directions." He made a whirlwind with his hands to show me what my energy felt like to him. His advice: lots more shiatsu.

After I dressed my body felt relaxed but my mind was just as tense. I returned to Nina's house and found her dancing with Brendan, bobbing him up and down to some fairly rowdy rock-and-roll songs. Nina had been studying the guitar.

I thanked her, admired her new pink Lady's Special electric, and reclaimed my son and the well-stocked diaper bag I had left. We chatted a bit as she brought toys inside from the porch. It had begun to look like rain. I told her that I had been up nights and that while the massage was pleasant enough I feared it had failed to cure me. She looked at me and said knowingly, "Remember, no matter how bad you feel, it never looks so bad from the outside. No one else will know if you don't tell them." She had written two books about becoming a mother. Then again, I had written one too.

I wasn't in therapy at the time. At the orientation meeting the year prior the director of our program had said with great, nearly intrusive gravity, "It is highly recommended that when you start learning to practice therapy, you be in some kind of therapy yourself to deal with the feelings that might be stirred up by clinical work. Many new clinicians find they need to work out issues around dependency, authority, and incomplete grief." The room went hush. All twenty-eight of us glanced around, half-accusingly, at the others: have *you* neglected to work out your issues and therefore run the risk of projecting your own problems on your clients?

Who me?! I had chuckled to myself, mindful of the decade or so I had on most of my fellow students, and determined that with all the years of therapy I had been through this was one school subject I could safely place out of. Indeed, I had been in analysis in New York during my twenties, foraging through my unconscious in an airless high-rise flat while construction on the Guggenheim Museum hammered on next door. Another year I drove 100 miles up I-95 every other week to see the therapist in Connecticut who had seen me through my miscarriage. Considering all that treatment I should probably get extra credit. But I now began to mentally flip through the memories of my previous therapies, like taking a well-worn reference book off the shelf, trying to tease out clues as to what was happening to me.

I silently refreshed myself about the details of my history as I had come to accept it in therapy: "A serious case of mumps before the age of two that left me feeling fragile... My mother caught it from me when she was pregnant with my brother, and it was feared that his subsequent vision problems were related to her illness ... Unconsciously felt I had "damaged" my brother and felt that my resentments towards the new baby had caused this... My paternal grandmother committed suicide when I was three, which I was never explicitly told about although it seemed I had always known. Somehow I might have felt that, like my brother's illness, this was my fault."

This basic narrative had been invoked to account for every emotional rough spot I hit: there's that unconscious stuff, kicking up again. It satisfied the clinicians I worked with as an explanation and therefore it satisfied me.

In my lone late-night hours I tried to apply that core story to what I was experiencing now. I couldn't make it work. I also tried to make it fit in with theories I was learning in grad school. This worked all too well: I realized I could be seen as having deficits in every essential line of development. It didn't take a psychoanalytic scholar to figure out that all those disruptive childhood events took place between the ages of one and three, the pivotal phase of separation/individuation (Margaret Mahler's term for the process of becoming an independent, secure person). I was clearly doomed. No wonder I was a mess.

Back then it never occurred to me to think in biological terms. No clinician had ever mentioned the term "mood disorder" to me and only once had a therapist even raised the possibility of a trial of medication, in that case to get me though a particularly tough spell. But at the time the cause of (now I know: *justification for*) my depression was that I was having trouble getting pregnant after suffering a miscarriage, and antidepressants weren't considered advisable for someone trying to conceive. I never gave medication another thought.

In principle I was against the idea of psychotropic medicine. That was a cop-out, I would think. I had a Puritan ethic of pain. As many of my notions of how to live my life had been formed in psychotherapy, I subscribed to a kind of therapy macho. I knew of people who hardly slept for months when their unconscious conflicts broke through, or who couldn't leave their room for days. "Medication," I would have scoffed had someone suggested it to me in earnest. "Why? Don't you think I can take the pain?" I may have been uncomfortable, even miserable, I told myself, but *at least I wasn't running away from things*. Nor was I looking for easy answers. This lent a sense of moral superiority that I could carry around like a protective shield.

In my masters program the topic of medication came up only within very specific contexts. Discussions of the biochemical and the psychodynamic took place in different lectures; in our textbooks they were in separate chapters if they appeared in the same book at all. There was no sense that a client might cross over from one realm to the other. I accepted the notion that mood disorders had discreet, definable symptoms that were very much in the present. In the training film we saw the "depressed person" was a sluggish, overweight woman who slept or lay around the house all day. After she went to a clinic and took medication she gained energy, lost weight, and got a job. Happy end of story. The "anxiety disorder" example was a man whose panic attacks started, without warning, while grocery shopping. The shopping in itself had no symbolic meaning; his father wasn't, to my knowledge, a grocer. Again, once treated with medication he was on his merry way.

Psychodynamic issues, on the other hand, concerned family relationships and events of the past, all the juicy stuff: the who's, the why's, and the wherefores. They drew on dreams and language and codes. Biological treatments were scientific and based on chemical formulas. Psychodynamic treatment was creative, intellectual, even aesthetic. A person fit one model or the other. It seemed clear to me how my case would be construed.

Throughout the fall I alternately tried to figure things out and to push unnerving ideas out of my head. As Christmas break approached I began to set sights on that stretch of vacation as a time to clear my head, focus on my family, and let things calm down inside.

* * *

The dominant mode of psychotherapy is dramatic irony. In a literary context, dramatic irony is when the reader (or audience, in a drama) understands the significance of what is happening or being said, but the character remains oblivious. It creates an irresistible suspense in any book, drama, or film. In *Some Like It Hot*, for example, *we* know that the "lady singers" are really men but Marilyn Monroe thinks they're a couple of lively gals. That's what makes dormitory and pajama-party scenes so hysterical. When and how will the truth come out, we wonder? And will it?

The concept of dramatic irony explains what goes on in a typical therapy session. The therapist is operating on the assumption that she knows the real (i.e. unconscious) import of what the client is saying. But the client is unaware of this. It is within that particular space, the interval between the facts and their unconscious meaning, that the therapist does her work, carefully linking the unconscious to everyday consciousness through the skillful use of language and observation.

The therapeutic dialogue occurs on several levels at the same time: the surface story ("manifest content," in the professional lingo); the underlying hypothesis which the therapist is using as a basis for her responses and interpretations; and the therapist's comments, through which the therapist is pushing the margins of the client's awareness of deeper feelings and motivations. Clinicians call this capacity to listen beyond the client's overt presentation "listening with the third ear" (from analyst Theodor Reik's phrase) much the way mystics talk of seeing with a third eye. Indeed, I believe you develop an ear for this material the way you might develop an ear for music or poetry.

In a good session you can keep the irony rolling for the better part of the hour, strategically crafting your comments so that everything you say refers to both the actual conversation you're having and the subterranean emotional/unconscious material. I say: "So, Lucy, you say you wanted to read last night, but you had so many books strewn about your bedroom that you didn't even know where to begin." I'm thinking: "I see you're feeling somewhat overwhelmed today."

When Lucy nods in agreement I can then say: "I wonder if there's a way to prioritize those books, so that at any given moment the task of choosing what to read isn't so daunting. Maybe you can put books that really grab you in a certain place, perhaps closest to your bed or desk, and you can reach for those first." Beneath the surface I am telling her: "Perhaps your internal world can be structured in such a way that your life feels more manageable." If there were an audience for this exchange, I would be winking in its direction.

Staying in the ironic vein creates a dramatic tension in the therapeutic dialogue. This was how it worked with Marta. Marta's father had largely been absent in the decade since the divorce. Her memories of him, greatly inflated through distance, were portrayed as loving and playful, qualities she felt lacking in her current life and certainly in her relationship with her mother.

My hypothesis was that much of Marta's ardent longing for romance represented a longing for her father. Whenever feelings about her father threatened to bubble to the surface she would immediately shift and start talking about her ex-boyfriend, Sam. "I miss Sam so much," she would sigh dreamily. "I know he feels the same way about me. I wish things hadn't gotten so complicated that we just can't be together."

I quickly caught on that to some extent Sam was an unconscious code for her father. Yes, things were "too complicated" for her to be with her father right now; any time Marta contacted her father her mother took this as a slap in the face and took this out on Marta. Also, Marta had built up her father to a level of perfection no man could meet. By keeping him in fantasy she could hold onto that vision of perfection and fend off potentially crushing disappointment. For these reasons discussing her relationship with her father directly was too fraught for Marta right now. So we talked about Sam. We talked about Sam's cryptic phone messages ("What does he mean, he'll 'see me over the weekend'? Is he planning on showing up at Sonya's party after all?"); we talked about Sam's charms ("he's so sensitive") and his shortcomings ("he's *too* sensitive"). And underneath all this we rummaged around Marta's heady, dream-driven relationship with her father. Indeed, amidst all of our "girl talk" the image of Marta's father, a spectral, teasing presence, hovered about the room.

For Ellen, "father" was less an object of romance than a source of struggle and frustration. Her father, a Viet Nam veteran who ran a small local electronics shop, drank a lot and was unreliable. The oldest of three children, Ellen made it a point to always be there for her family. Ellen said that she was furious with her father *not* because he drank but because he wouldn't admit he had an alcohol problem. She was now playing out her ongoing battle with her father through her stormy relationship with Jack, her boss at the department store, who had hired and rehired her several times over the past year or so.

At one point Ellen quit in the middle of a major sales promotion. "It serves him right," she said, crossing her arms defiantly. "He was pushing me. He knew there was no way I could handle everything he asked me to do unless I worked late every night. And he knew that I would work late every night if that's what needed to be done. Well I'm through with being dependable. He can find someone else to depend on."

Referring both to the boss and, indirectly, to her father, I said: "Why do you feel he should bear the brunt of your frustration?"

She sighed, "I don't know. There's just a certain kind of self-centered middle-aged guy that I find impossible to deal with." She scrunched up her nose, an expression of irritation and disgust.

When you're using dramatic irony in a session, it's particularly powerful when you can get the two levels — the day-to-day and the unconscious — to converge. I could tell Ellen was drifting away from the emotional content by intellectualizing, talking vaguely about "middle-aged guys". So I decided to take our conversation to the emotional realm. I said: "I wonder if your frustration isn't really about this particular work situation but about how he (intentionally leaving who "he" represents ambiguous) has treated you and what that has meant to you."

"Yes." Ellen then stopped short. "I'm sorry. What did you say?"

Me: "Well, it's clear that you are important to him."

Ellen: "But I would never know that from how he treats me."

Me: "Yes."

Ellen: "But I've been dealing with this kind of thing all of my life," her voice beginning to soften with feeling.

Me: "That's right. You have."

That's right, she had. Here the two realms come together and the irony disbands.

I saved up every last trifle from my sessions to share with Bonnie on Monday. I *adored* Bonnie. I felt utterly taken care of by her, sure of her wisdom. I had never before had a true mentor, someone totally committed to my development. I responded to that devotion, working to please her as well as help my clients. I was like a schoolgirl waiting for the approving pat on the head. I loved the feeling of lapping up new knowledge from someone I admired. Our meetings were intense. With scarcely a hello, Bonnie would hang up her coat and scurry to her desk, a mug of coffee cradled in both hands. I would be sitting, my notebook already open to the page and ready to begin. So much material, so little time.

                        * * *

Right after my last Saturday session of the term Tony, Brendan and I flew to San Diego to spend the holidays with my mother-in-law, Liesel. I kept expecting to relax but I didn't. I couldn't. I was on overdrive, plain and simple, and could not change gears. In fact, the only difference in my state of mind was, aside from the shakiness I already felt, the added irreality of feeling warm in the Southern California sun despite the winter light. All the exhaustion I banked up through the fall failed to score me a night's sleep. In the late afternoons we observed the daily official state holiday — the sunset — but to me day and night were blurred so it was merely a visual display, out of context. Mornings Liesel would come out in her robe and find me at the breakfast table staring idly at the newspaper. She'd ask, "Did you have a good night?" Did she really want to know?

One day I went to visit my friend Barb. I wore one of my therapist outfits, a brightly-colored light wool jacket over slim black jeans. I tried to summon the confident cool of my therapist persona. I stood in Barb's backyard, hands in my stylish angled pockets, while she talked of her garden and the coyotes that come up from the canyon at night and I told her all about my new career.

"That's so cool what you're doing," she said, bending down to pinch a sprig of rosemary. "I barely get a chance to even read a book with two kids and a dog."

"And a bird."

"Not to mention a guinea pig. And — almost forgot — a husband. You're so good at focusing and getting things done. I admire that."

"Oh, it's really nothing..."

I seemed to have it all together. But this conjuring act was unconvincing,

at least to myself.

I felt jumpy (restless, distracted, spent, pounding and tightness in my chest) but kept telling myself that everything was okay. For wasn't everything okay? Here I was with my family and my kindly mother-in-law, getting a well-deserved break from my work in a beautiful place with arguably the best weather you could find in this country at the tail end of December. What wouldn't be okay?

We did what we always do on San Diego's north coast: we walk. We walk to glittering, shamelessly overpriced shops and to our favorite café, a place where they switch from heaters to umbrellas depending on the sun and where babies and dogs are welcome (home-baked dog biscuits for a quarter). We walk along the beach. We walk high on the cliffs and we admire them from below. These are the same fine, dramatic cliffs that inspired Dr. Seuss's fantastical landscapes, cliffs that can look anywhere from deep brown to bright pink depending on the light.

One afternoon we started on beach level and climbed up the rocks to Torrey Pines State Park, known for its views and unique sea-battered trees. This was the park where just a year before we had decided on the name Brendan, partly as a near anagram of Bernard, Tony's grandfather's name, and partly because we saw beautiful ravens and Brendan means raven in Gaelic.

We were hiking at a nice, easy pace, and I watched our son in his bright blue Tough Traveler pack, gently bouncing up and down on my husband's back. I could see Tony's sure feet moving among the rocks as I scrambled along just a few steps behind. Suddenly I became horrifyingly aware of how hard these rocks were and how far from ground level we had climbed. Oh my God — it would be so easy to fall!

What would happen to the baby? How could we protect him? Should we be up here at all? Where would he be totally safe? I kept walking, breathless, as though by keeping going I could outpace this new fear.

I was alarmed — terror-stricken — but I wasn't sure about what. Was I worried my husband would drop Brendan? I didn't think so; I had always trusted Tony and that trust had never been misplaced nor faltered. Was I worried I would drop him? This last concern seemed the more reasonable one. But I wasn't even the one carrying him. How had I mindlessly gone on, toting around this fragile infant all these months? What hazards there were when I thought about it. What had I been thinking?

I couldn't get this idea out of my head. It started a painful, continuous loop in my mind. What if, I kept wondering? *What if?*

Before I had been edgy. Now I was *unstrung*. I felt anxiety that only went away when I felt sad or cried. The sadness, then, could be relieved only by the adrenalin boost another jolt of anxiety gave me. And on it went. I couldn't understand why an idea that barely made a dent in my consciousness one minute could nearly paralyze me the next. Now I was so scared *for* my child it was almost that I felt scared *of* him. Can I touch him? Will I break him? My emotions were all twisted up in knots, my confidence as a mother completely smashed.

This was clearly a kind of panic attack, some overloading of the neural circuits, but back then I didn't see it that way. It was also merely a more extreme version of the up-and-down swings I had always contended with. I had always had a fear of being out of control. Acknowledging my child's fragility and dependence on me gave a palpable scenario to the fear.

Because this anguish bore a familiar tinge I sought out a familiar solution. I started leafing through those old memories again, hoping to retrieve a revealing scene or a telling phrase from some previous therapy. Freud had famously said, "Hysterics [read: neurotics or others in emotional pain] suffer mainly from reminiscences." There had to be something back there. I imagined that there was some intuitive connection that needed to be made, like flipping over a concealed card.

I put in a call to my Chicago therapist, Linda, a hip and highly-regarded psychiatrist who had been pleased with my growth over the year I had spent in her care, and we arranged a session over the phone. Across the wires we unbundled my psychic material and Linda linked this current impasse to my early childhood illness and fears of damaging my brother as a child. She attributed my current anxiety I was feeling now to the fear that everything would go wrong again and that I would somehow be punished. "Maybe you feel guilty about being happy," she suggested.

"Maybe so," I replied.

We decided to meet again when I returned to Chicago.

Session over. *Click.*

She's brilliant, I thought, lamenting the unconscious time bomb that had been lurking in my head all those years. I thought I had done enough psychotherapy to cleanse my unconscious sufficiently to raise a child. I thought I had done enough psychotherapy to handle anything. I grieved over the apparent inevitability of this crisis, and hoped that Linda would be able to ferry me through it with dispatch. I was ready to put myself in her able hands.

⁑ ⁑ ⁑

Happily, my clients weathered the holiday break far better than I did. Each seemed pleased to see me and to report on the progress in her life.

In mid-December, Ellen had started a new job in a dental office that was going well. She earned enough that she could move out of her parent's house and into her own apartment. (I was concerned how she would budget her money, however, and mentally filed that question away.) She was wearing a smart navy blue wool coat and had styled her hair differently. I commented on that, and it was nice to see how she brightened under attention.

Marta had dreaded Christmas, recalling endless dreary days in her mother's house, listening to her mother complain about her life and feeling guilty that she couldn't make her happy. Before the break we had discussed how she might make the visit more pleasant. Now she proudly

31

told me that she had invited several friends, including her male roommate, to her mother's house for a long weekend. "We had a great time!" she said. "Everybody pitched in. We made some wacky meals — turkey *mole* instead of roast turkey — and my friends were able to drag my mother out of her *mood*."

With Lucy it was more subtle. She was rather noncommittal about her holiday ("Oh, it was okay") but I sensed that something was happening. As I brought her from the waiting room to my office I thought, "Lucy looks pretty today. I never noticed what a nice, fresh complexion she has." Before I could shape this observation into an appropriate comment, Lucy said, "Hey, I like what you're wearing. What do you call that kind of wool again, mohair is it?" It was as though some bit of good feeling, a spark of warmth and connection, had flitted between us, gracing one and then the other.

"Yes it is," I said, smiling, as we walked in the door. "And thank you."

In training there's a lot of talk about making good use of your "self". As a psychotherapist what you've got to work with is, essentially, yourself. Your self is your instrument.

In clinical terms, the notion of self is a bit more complicated than that which makes you, *you*. It's more of a constellation of experiences, attributes, and motivations that make up a given person's psychological essence. As a therapist in a therapy setting, you are not merely you. You are also a conglomeration of psychological functions to be employed in the service of your client. You call upon different parts of yourself as needed. When Bonnie wrote on an evaluation that I showed "a flexible use of self" she meant I was doing adapting my clinical strategy to different clients.

Here's how this works in practice: if a client is overly distraught about something or having trouble coping, you might want to "lend" that person your ego. In other words, you are offering your sense of reality for him or her to lean on.

This is what I sometimes did in my work with Ellen. She had a tendency to act impulsively. When we started in September, she had that retail job she hated. Specifically, she hated her boss, Jack, who she felt was condescending to her even though she was the first person he always turned to. Sometimes she would come to a session and rant, "I don't 'take order's. I'm a professional and I expect to be treated as a professional." One day, after a department manager had complained to Jack about her handling of a customer, Ellen declared that she was going to quit.

Maybe Jack was patronizing to Ellen. But it wasn't clear to me that quitting was Ellen's best move when she had bills to pay and no other prospects. So I slowed her down and helped her look at the facts. When Ellen left that session she said she wasn't going to go in and throw her employee badge on the sales counter after all. She was going to go home and think about her options first. In the end, she didn't leave the job until a few weeks later when she had the position at the dentist's office lined up.

Another use of self involved maintaining a clear boundary between myself and a client so that I could resist being pulled into a problematic symbiosis. I would use my own critical faculty to remain distinct from my client and thus offer her a different model for relating to people in her life.

For example, Marta was a very seductive client in that she was so easy to be around. During our appointments I sometimes found myself in the mind of Saturday mornings drinking tea with girlfriends during my early 20s, our feet up on the couch, trying to make sense of the men we knew. It was hard not to get swept up in Marta's romantic dramas for their soap opera value. ("And Sam said *what*?! You're kidding!") Gee, this is a pleasant way to spend an hour, I might think. ("Hey, did I ever tell you about the time a guy tried to pull that one on me?" I'd be tempted to say. "I'll take a little milk in that tea, please...")

Whoa — I'd catch myself. This is *countertransference*, a therapist's personal response to the client. Marta needed another buddy like, well, she needed another hole in the head (with those piercings and all). Her mother always treated her like a chum; if mom wanted someone to talk to, she'd tie up Marta's phone line all night even if it meant telling Marta upsetting things about her current boyfriend or Marta's dad. So I would pull back and play a different role for Marta. I then make a different use of my self — that of emotional gatekeeper.

When you insert yourself into your client's sessions you joggle her reality somewhat. You're tossing a wild card into her story. It's as though, in a novel, an omniscient narrator were whispering into the main character's ear. Or as if you could walk right into the book and make things different.

You see, in psychotherapy you can. By engaging with the client in a way that teaches her a new way to experience or understand a situation, you can help her alter her behavior and avoid making the same mistakes. If we all go through much of our lives on psychological automatic pilot, therapy puts the system on hold. You, the therapist, come in like a backup generator, assuming certain tasks as the client begins to readjust.

The idea is that the new style of behavior will be more successful. It will feel better to Ellen to competently manage a conflict at work than to lash out and be stuck with the consequences. It will feel better to Marta to choose whom to be intimate with and to be able to enjoy some autonomy. In theory, the client will "internalize" the function that you have provided for them. Ellen will learn to do her own reality checking. Marta will learn to be her own gatekeeper.

It was gratifying to see that I could use my "self" to help my clients grow. I began to hear Ellen say things like, "I was going to yell at my brother for leaving his junk in my car, but then I thought: wait a second. I'm in a bad mood and he's in a bad mood and it wouldn't do anyone any good. So I went upstairs and took a bubble bath."

That pause, that "wait a second", is the therapist's contribution. That's the omniscient narrator gripping the character by the lapels and saying, "Is this really the direction you want the story to take?"

I was awed by how I could lend my own strengths and insights to benefit my clients. I was also confounded by how I could not make that same command available to myself.

*　*　*

I resumed therapy with Linda. She was a warm, pleasant woman who wore her wavy gray hair down, constantly pushing it over her ear like a teenager. She had the lean, calm look of someone who did yoga every day. But things did not work out as I had hoped. According to Linda, everything was basically fine with me and this episode of shakiness was just a minor setback. She suggested that perhaps I somehow needed to "check back" with what I had been through so that I could then move on with greater clarity and conviction. She had apparently seen this pattern frequently.

"Remember all those months when you wondered whether you would be able to conceive a child at all?" Her eyes nearly misted as she recollected the main themes of our work together two years earlier. "Well you did, and now you have this wonderful little boy that you're so happy with. You're hitting a rough spot and you're wondering if you'll get past it. *Of course* you will. Look at what you've done! You're a mother and you've become a therapist at the same time! You know what it's like to be in pain and you know what it's like to be happy. That is a very powerful combination. Give yourself some credit."

I wanted to believe Linda but I couldn't. Sure, everything *was* going well. But I wasn't okay. I knew that. And by this point I was no longer just jittery. I was now feeling relentless, consuming pain. I kept myself busy, trying to out-race it. But the second I failed to fully distract myself, the pain would rear up again.

This pain was more intense than the kind of low-level churning I could rationalize (loneliness, grieving a miscarriage, getting used to a new part of the country, the weather...) It had a higher frequency. If it had a sound, it would be in the upper registers. For a while the feeling *did* seem to have a sound. I would become hyper-aware of background noise, as though the pain was outside of me and I could move toward it or away from it but never escape it completely. I would dread being in a room with a loud heating system because my mind would zero in on it. At home I tried to position myself beyond hearing range of the refrigerator going on and off, on and off. This was extremely disconcerting, to say the least. I wondered if I was going crazy.

I told Bonnie about this symptom and asked, as casually as I could: "Have you ever come across anything like this before?"

"Not exactly, but I've heard of other disconcerting symptoms," she said.

On the one hand, I wanted it affirmed that what I was experiencing was miserable beyond the normal scale of misery. On the other, I wanted to be reassured that I *wasn't* crazy.

I talked to Tony. "What do you think is going on?" I asked.

"Maybe having new work and a new baby is more stressful than you realize."

"But I'm happy with the baby. And I'm happy with the work."

"I know."

"Do you think it's more of the same old psychological baggage?"

"I don't know. I wouldn't know. Can't Linda help you there?" He approved of Linda. She was, as I said, hip and smart.

"I don't know. I hope so."

Tony never criticized me for needing therapy; his complete acceptance of me always stunned me. This acceptance went both ways. We always supported each other and put up with our respective forms of nonsense. When Tony and I got married, on the night the clocks turn back so we could have the extra hour, our private vows were to "love, honor, and humor each other." If he had to abide my endless self-analysis, so be it. I fooled myself and told myself this reflected personal depth. I think Tony fooled himself about it too. I tried not to take his tolerance for granted, but sometimes I did.

I also knew that I had at times over-involved my husband in my problems. It was hard for me not to; I was so overwhelmed. I wanted to avoid doing this. One reason I had been in therapy in recent years was to become less dependent on him. When Tony and I first got together, I kidded myself with the delusion that love itself could subdue chronic malaise. For a while it had seemed enough. Although a writer, Tony was spared the classic artist's temperament; he is as solid and clear-minded as anyone I know. He takes imaginative flight, to be sure, but from a strong base. For a long time I would try to tuck myself into his very being, playing psychological tag-along with him, sort of like "He's okay so I must be okay." But this wasn't working anymore. By seeing a therapist, I could learn how to be more resilient. At the very least, someone else could handle some of the emotional overflow so that Tony wasn't constantly deluged.

That was the idea, anyway. When I was in therapy, Tony had to hear not only about my problems, but also about my *breakthroughs.* Sometimes in a session or on my own I would experience an epiphany. This might be on the order of: due to my grandmother's suicide, my family has been in an arrested state of mourning; or, because of my early envy of my brother I have always felt guilty that I wanted too much. Each revelation would add a new twist to the plot line, allowing me to recast the story in a fresh light, lending some details added significance while letting others drop to the background.

I couldn't resist sharing my new discoveries with Tony. "*Now* I understand why being alone has always been so uncomfortable to me. After all those years..." I might be disconnected, distracted, or up a lot at night while I was interpreting these new insights and was not much fun to be around. But more than anything he wished for me to find a degree of inner peace. A loving husband and good listener, he took at face value my conviction that I was truly getting somewhere, and was continually being dragged into my internal world while being yanked out of his own.

With me feeling worse, Linda and I added sessions when we could. I would take the same lumbering elevated train that I took when I went to the Agency, stopping in a posh shopping district a few blocks from the lake. Within a given week I might switch several times from being the clinician to being client, from the bearer of reassurance and understanding to the recipient of it. One day I would head downtown to help others put their lives together; the next I would trek there to try to hold myself together. I scrambled to add babysitting hours.

After a few weeks of jovial chit-chat about clinical training and new motherhood interspersed with long private stretches of unremitting dread, I found that I couldn't conform to Linda's preferred script. I was plainly too shaky and needed more continual contact with a therapist to bolster me, like an intravenous drip.

What I know now: my biochemistry had gone totally haywire and I needed to be on medication if I was to get better.

What I thought then: I needed more psychological exploration to work through the unconscious material that had been stirred up through practicing therapy and becoming a mother.

I did not want to be in this place. I wanted to be in the world. I didn't want to be in my head; I had dwelled there enough. I was tired of putting my life on hold. I was tired of telling Tony that our lives were on hold. ("Really, love, I won't *always* get so unhinged by… *Fill in the blank*:

1) brief or significant absences
2) my family
3) *your* family
4) daily life

I just need to work out some of this psychological stuff first. Just bear with me for a bit longer…")

Truly, the last thing I wanted was to be mucking around in my unconscious. I wanted to devote myself to my child and my husband, but my attention was drawn more and more inward to the minutiae of emotional memory. What was the hidden source of this persisting pain? Was I lacking in some primal nurturing way back when? Was I assigned the role as "the bad one" in my family and internalized this negative image of myself?

For this last notion, thanks to graduate school, I now had a spanking new term to explain it: *projective identification*. (Projective identification: Unwanted aspects of the self are deposited into another person… The defense allows one to distance and make oneself understood by exerting pressures on another person to experience feelings similar to one's own. *Kaplan and Sadock's Synopsis of Psychiatry*.) In other words, "internalizing the role of the bad one" allowed me to serve as a kind of dumping ground for all the bad feelings in my family.

How might this have worked? Like this: my father undoubtedly had a great deal of pain, guilt, sadness, and regret surrounding his mother's suicide. That plus anger at his own father for being aloof and unsupportive, and perhaps resentment towards his brother who, born when my father was eight, he had helped to raise. These feelings were so uncomfortable and so at odds with how he wanted to perceive himself that he unconsciously "gave" them to me, treating me as if I had those feelings until, ultimately, I experienced myself as I did.

Likewise my mother, brought up in many ways like a precious doll in a wealthy, nearly old-world home, liked to present herself as a "good girl". As no girl is all good she, at least theoretically, severed her rages, envies, and un-good-girl-like desires and lobbed them my way so that she could be all-good and I would be all-bad. This latter example is called "splitting", as in splitting the good from the bad.

This is a tidy and convenient way to keep feelings in the family without having to feel any of them. There is, though, a steep psychological cost: the person who becomes the repository of those feelings is stuck with them, and those who jettisoned them have to continually work to stave them off. And all this occurs beneath the level of consciousness.

Was this brand of mental gymnastics fun? Hardly. Did I believe this was going to help me get better? Yes. Was I desperate enough to believe in any framework that promised me relief? Without a doubt. At least it helped focus my restless mind; the theoretical permutations were endless.

Linda regretted that she wasn't set up to do the kind of depth work that I wanted to do and which required several appointments a week. We parted ways. "I do wish you well," she said, offering a commiserating look and a slender hand.

A clinician associated with my masters program gave me the phone number of a woman she thought I might work well with. Not only was this Dr. Hammond said to be skillful and sensitive; her office was just ten minutes from my house.

I put a call in to Dorothy Hammond, Ph.D. and she mercifully got back to me within a couple of hours. I immediately liked her. In our brief phone conversation I described what I was experiencing. I even told her about the annoying symptom of constantly hearing background noise — an ever-present mechanical hum — that gave me the feeling that pain and anxiety was surrounding me.

She paused, and in a calm, gentle voice said, "It sounds as if you don't feel *safe.*"

"Yes!" I exclaimed, overwhelmed by gratitude. *Brilliant.* Finally, someone really understands me. I felt safer already.

*   *   *

I began to look forward to my Saturday sessions as a distraction from my own unease. For a few hours I could count on being transported away from myself because it was, after all, my job. For the better part of a day I could dress myself up in a fashionable outfit and exercise some competence in the professional world. The connection I made with my clients was powerful and gratifying, an island amidst drift.

We were now deep into winter. My clients would come in shivering, and take a few moments to thaw out and peel off layers of outerwear. Still, the direct morning light in the office remained strong. I usually got the chance to make the nominal maternal gesture of adjusting the blinds so that my clients would be comfortable.

We were also now deep into our collaborative work. Each of my clients had begun to anticipate what I might say in a given situation, and use this new inner voice as a vehicle for her growth.

"You would have been proud of me," Lucy said one day. "I saw a poster about a free lecture at the Art Institute. First of all, I wrote it down in my calendar and didn't lose track of it." She flicked a finger and drew an imaginary point in the air. "And then I actually got myself ready and out of my apartment in time to get there early enough to get a seat. It was a nice thing to do. Now I feel more motivated to do things in this city, not because I'm *supposed* to but because I want to. A lot of cool people seem to go to these things."

"You won't believe this," Ellen said as we started a session. "I had to go to see Jack about some check I hadn't received. I remembered what we had talked about, you know, how he did appreciate me even though it was hard for me to see it, and we had a pleasant-enough conversation. I probably will end up contacting him again for a reference, or even fill-in work, like around big sales or Christmas."

Sometimes a shift can be perceived by others, even if it's unarticulated. In one session Marta mentioned in passing, "I was talking to my mother on the phone and she said that I sounded busy and so she would let me go. She didn't say it in a way that I should feel guilty or anything, she just got off the phone. I thought that was a kind of neat thing."

I was excited about this work. And in theory at least, I was happy with my life. Certainly there were moments when everything did seem to be in balance. I remember one evening Tony and I invited Nina over for dinner. It was Saturday night; the week paused to let us catch our breath. The wind from Lake Michigan was bitterly cold but we were warmed by the curry Tony had cooked and the oil lamps that lent light to the table. Nina brought the wine, Greek as was our custom. I could hear Brendan snorting pleasantly from his bedroom.

We talked about our writing projects, all in varying stages of incompletion, and I told of the parallels I was finding between writing and doing psychotherapy. "Character really does determine fate," I said. "It's amazing."

I described the sorts of stories I might encounter from week to week, the events that seemed plucked from fate to match each client's need for growth, the inner transformations suggested or revealed. Tony was teaching beginning fiction at the time and he admitted to envy over the rich material I got compared with the more contrived, too-neatly-devised stories that came across his desk.

Nina agreed. "What great stuff to work with. Hey, that's neat that you say metaphors get woven through the treatment. I never thought about how that process would be from the therapist's point of view."

"You know, I looked up the word metaphor and the definition I found was 'transference', I said, on a roll now. "Isn't that interesting, given that the notion of transference — where the patient responds *as if* the therapist were someone important from the past, like a parent — is so central to psychotherapy?"

"You know sometimes I've thought that if I wanted to do something other than writing the things I'd most consider would be getting chef's training or learning to do psychotherapy," Nina said. "I can't think of anything else I'd get excited about. So, do you miss writing at all right now?"

"Not at the moment," I said, giving her my stock response. "I'm getting my "story fix" with my work."

"I bet you could write something about all this."

"Maybe I will."

I was excited about all that I was discovering. I was proud of what I had been able to do for my clients. In some small, bright corner of my mind I could hear myself observe: "You know, Judy, things are really pretty good right now." I even repeated this observation, for my own benefit: "Yes, things are really quite okay."

"Hold it right there — " I said to myself, like a photographer who has caught the perfect pose and doesn't want to lose it. *Hold* that internal pose. Keep it in your mind for reference. Know that such states of well-being are possible.

Even as I clasped this thought I knew that this contentment would elude me other than in the most fleeting way. I savored its pleasing sensation, like our meal.

*　*　*

At nine o'clock on a Thursday morning I had my first appointment with Dr. Hammond. I spent the night before awake with palpitations (generalized anxiety, oh God just get through the night). She greeted me and her expectant expression invited me to talk. I'm all over the place: the persistent sounds (take them away), the feelings (take them too), my son, my husband, my writing (I sense a whirlwind...)

As I began to run out of steam she offered some advice. "I notice that you are very tuned into your child," she said. "Caring for him seems to bring you back to yourself. Your love for him grounds you. Focus on your baby. That will help to center you." The racing heart persisted throughout the day, but I kept myself focused on Brendan (not that I needed a shrink to tell me that, with all due respect), bouncing him against my hip as we waited in a miniscule examining room for a well-child visit, blowing kisses at him as we rolled down supermarket aisles. By the time evening came I relaxed and, blessedly, slept.

I quickly grew accustomed to Dr. Hammond's cozy little office, a sunny square of worn-but-homey furnishings located off the long, dark, corridor of an office building. Next to her desk, framed school photos leaned against the requisite professional books, many of which were now familiar to me. (Were there two little boys or was that just the same boy at different ages?) Dr. Hammond was tall and a bit heavy, in an athletic sort of way, but dressed as a more petite woman would: short jackets, tailored blouses, and the like. I often wondered when, with her clinical work and a family, she found the time to shop. We created a regular schedule: Thursday morning and Monday afternoon. My hours. Inviolable.

I warmed up to her clinical style. She had a friendly, empathetic manner, and a way of narrowing her eyes when she thought an idea or comment worth pursuing. There was a quiet sternness about her which made me feel that whatever darknesses remained at large — and if I was still in so much pain there *must* be some pretty bleak stuff in there — wouldn't be too much for her to handle.

Dr. Hammond also seemed interested in me. She seemed to have respect for my being a writer, which made me feel I carried some weight with her. (This was probably my fantasy. No doubt she was simply allying with my strengths — another Counseling 101 guideline.) I decided that she was a good person for me to work with right now. No, I went beyond that: I imagined that in some cosmic way she was *the* right person to work with.

As I calmed down a bit and our meetings became routine, we began to discuss plans for our work together. (Of course, one must always have a treatment plan.) I laid it on the line for her: "Everything in my life is fine," I explained. "My parents aren't perfect but I can accept them. I have a lovely family, satisfying, creative work and good friends. The problem is me." I described the consistent current of pain that had run the entire length of my life. I shared with her the sense that I was not so much living my days as managing them. I described a constant sense of inner wobbliness, as though the world itself wasn't enough to sustain me. I went on, relating the details of my history with the rote assurance of someone who has explained herself to many prospective employers or to innumerable blind dates.

Dr. Hammond offered affirmation for what I was going through. "Perhaps it's the clinical training, perhaps it's the intensity of new motherhood, or perhaps it's your age, being in your mid-30s," she said, leaning forward over stout, nylon-clad knees. "Whatever it is you are clearly ready to take this inner journey and become what you can be, experiencing the full range of your emotions." She looked at me with sympathy bordering on pity; I was apparently quite effective in conveying how wretched and unevolved I was.

"But I'm not looking for a journey," I said, breaking her gaze. "I just want to be okay where I am."

Again: I didn't want to be in this place. I had spent enough time on my own problems. They weren't even that interesting. I had a lot to be thankful for. I wanted to give back to others now. It was time.

"People don't always have control over when this material comes up. But it comes up when you're ready," she said, adding, "Many people never have the courage to go through this."

That caught my attention. Did I have courage? I didn't think so. Did I have a choice? It didn't seem that I did. Not if I ever wanted to feel like a whole person instead of a fragmented muddle.

She clearly picked up that the desperation I exuded didn't represent the totality of who I was. She was particularly alert to the discrepancy between who I was and how I experienced myself. I'm sure she got some sense of my competence as a new clinician, my level of insight and the degree of my caring. She saw that I could be light-hearted or witty, when so inclined, and that I had a strong marriage and good relationships in general. In sum, there was nothing so terribly wrong with me, once you totally disregarded how I felt.

Dr. Hammond's confidence in me lent me strength. She seemed to view my faltering mental state as an indication of *health*, a sign that I was ready to confront something important and true. Believing her made me feel that the tiny thread of hope I clung to was something that I could actually grasp. It also gave me pride; it seemed that lots of folks out there were secretly miserable but too oblivious or afraid to take the psychotherapeutic plunge and understand why. Maybe I did have courage after all.

One important thing, Dr. Hammond said, was to acknowledge the anger I was feeling toward Linda. I well knew that withheld and un-worked-through anger was psychologically damaging. Did I feel anger towards Linda? I didn't think so. But I was a mess. How would I know what I was feeling anyway?

A key theme in our work was the idea that I needed to learn to "soothe myself". Dr. Hammond referred to basic child development. First the infant needs a caretaker to do the soothing. Then, with maturation, the young child is able to soothe him- or herself. The child learns to soothe himself by using "transitional objects", D.W. Winnicott's term for those things that act as a bridge to independence, such as a baby blanket, stuffed animals, and the like. Rather than clinging to Mommy, a child carries around a favorite Teddy Bear. In time he can give up Teddy too. As far as I could recall I had never been able to soothe myself. Where was I the day transitional objects were handed out?

I told Dr. Hammond about how Brendan calmed himself by sucking his thumb. This had never bothered me. I rather fancied he looked debonair with his thumb in his mouth, thinking he conducted this habit with expression and aplomb. I noted that the nice thing about a thumb is that, unlike a pacifier, it is always available and he can't drop it on the floor. Dr. Hammond agreed.

"Do you mean to say that if I had, say, sucked my thumb when I was a young child I might not have the kind of constant discomfort that I do now?"

"Maybe." This seemed a theoretically viable possibility.

"Great. This whole thing is confounding to me because I can soothe others. I can do that in my work as a clinician. I can soothe my child."

"Then we know that the capacity for you to soothe yourself is there."

Our broad goal was for me to build that self-soothing capacity and be able to walk through the world without feeling like I was stumbling every few feet. I made it clear that I had never had a solid sense of self like I imagined most people did and Dr. Hammond said, with reassuring conviction, "I am going to ally myself with your strongest self and together we will build that inner core."

The means that would accomplish this was the same that I relied on in the work that I did with my clients: providing a "corrective emotional experience." The basic idea was this: an emotionally charged situation would come up and the therapist would handle it in a helpful, affirming way. This would undo whatever damage had occurred when the same situation was *mis*handled in the past and therefore free the client to respond more adaptively.

For example, let's say I felt afraid of something, say being alone. Dr. Hammond would empathize with that fear rather than denying it, as we theorized my early caretakers had done (how else to explain the magnitude of my fears?). She would emphasize her availability, making the point that as she was emotionally there for me I was never really alone. She would then help me cope with the fear in a way that allowed me to gain mastery over the situation.

This process is like a psychological revision. It alters the story. A situation or type of encounter that has always been threatening, difficult, or explosive is no longer so. Through the mechanism of transference, the corrective experience speaks directly to the guardian of narrative within each of us, the unconscious.

Now that, thanks to my training, I felt I understood the theory behind what we were doing, I was excited. But I was also apprehensive. What if I couldn't handle the feelings or memories that were unleashed? Dr. Hammond assured me that nothing would come up unless I was ready to handle it.

But those feelings, that diffuse but continual sense of the world as a menacing place, were so old, so intrinsic to me, I protested. She looked me straight in the eye and said: "You and I will be working together for a long time." There was that sternness. It put me a bit on edge but reassured me that she was in control. I could simply submit to her clinical wisdom.

Dr. Hammond went on to say that she didn't think I would discover anything new. What she meant was that I wouldn't be learning anything about my past that I didn't already know. "You have made a good start on this work before," she said, "but this time you might experience some of your history in a new way. The way I work is that I take people on a journey, wherever that person needs to go."

I set aside any doubts. My other therapies, even my analysis — where I lay on the couch and did the whole bit — were just warm-ups. This was the *real thing*. I believed that with her vast knowledge and experience, she knew what lay beneath my emotional pain. It was now up to me to be able to understand it, first intellectually and then viscerally. Dr. Hammond and I were a team. Freud, I recently learned, preferred to call his patients "students". As I was a student of therapy undergoing therapy, Dr. Hammond became a kind of ur-teacher with me learning at her feet. It made my treatment feel like the therapy of all therapies. Yes, I was ready to tackle my story, and to really get through it once and for all. No more taking it page by page, depending on where the book falls open. As a clinician and mother, I owed it to my clients and my son as well as myself. Making this commitment felt like a brave, even noble, thing to do.

✻　✻　✻

Back at graduate school, we trainees met every Tuesday morning as a class. My classmates impressed me. They spoke about emotion with the casual directness of office shoptalk. I might overhear, for example, someone discuss how she needed to "grieve the loss of a previous clinical placement" or that a conflict with a demanding supervisor was "touching on her issues". I was forever marveling at how on top of their psychological states they all seemed to be. As a group my classmates were bright Midwesterners, mostly women, with a palpable stability beyond their years. They were matter-of-fact about most of what they confronted in their therapy placements, but with their youthful enthusiasm and crisp career clothes seemed oddly untouched by life.

I liked my classmates but felt distant from them. How could it be otherwise? They were thinking about dating, while I was watching the clock to see when I needed to pump breast milk. Some high-voltage break-ups and pairings were going on within the group but these went right over my head.

The one thing most were gifted at was empathy. Indeed, empathy was the cornerstone of the program. At one point the director said, "If there is one thing I want you to take away from this program it's the importance of empathy." Someone with a knack for empathy can seem to understand something that may in fact be beyond his or her intellectual grasp. Or, through an expression or simple tilt of the head, be able to convert concern into reassurance. When presenting a case to the class, it was considered good form to tear up as you describe what the client was feeling. This was a sure sign of empathy. And then this gave the others a chance to empathize with *you*. Outright bawling, which is what I often felt like doing (though on my own behalf, not my clients') would not have been okay. Because emotion was always on the verge of breaching the surface, I kept my feelings under a tight lid.

As my experience was so far off the map I needn't have worried too much. While we were walking on campus, notebooks in hand, a classmate asked me how things were going. Do I tell? "Actually," I said, "things are kicking up a bit and I'm back in therapy — "

"I know *just* what you mean," she confided. "I'm always locking horns with my supervisor. I have real issues with authority. I've just started seeing a therapist here in town to try to work them out."

Oh, you have issues with authority? That sounds serious. Actually, I'm trying to work out my issues with *life*.

One thing drummed into us every Tuesday was to develop empathy for ourselves. "It's easy to burn out when you're beginning as a therapist," our teacher warned. "You need to find ways to take care of yourselves."

* * *

Psychotherapy can be a rocky process. It can be rocky for the therapist as well. As a clinician you can find yourself caught short or outright humbled.

One day Ellen threw a jab at a vulnerable spot — my self-assurance as a starting clinician. In supervision, Bonnie had made the point that a client may feel hurt or sad about a scheduled break in the treatment but not know how to articulate this. I should raise the topic, then, to give clients a chance to address those feelings. In anticipation of a vacation I said to Ellen, "Some people may find a break in therapy difficult. If you feel you need to get in touch with me — "

"HA!" she said, her voice tinged with savage glee. "Do you think that it's going to be so tough for me to not see *you* for a week or two?"

No doubt betraying my embarrassment, I quickly regrouped and said, "It might not be a problem for you, but, I mean, *some people do* find it somewhat challenging, and — "

Sometimes you inadvertently find yourself playing into your client's hand. For example, Lucy could be demanding. When she didn't like something she was not subtle about making her displeasure known. If I made a suggestion that didn't suit her, like most things that took effort on her part, she would make a face not unlike an eight-year-old child saying "*Yuck!*" I wanted to please her so I would dance around, trying to come up with something that satisfied her, trying to give Lucy her money's worth.

Typically she would dump a complaint on me as if to say, "There's the problem. I don't like it. Now *you* take care of it!" For example she'd say, "I haven't been able to get to the Art Institute again since that one time." Pause. So what are you going to do about that?

I'd say, "Why don't you go into work a little early on days there are lectures or events and make sure that you can leave the office on time?"

She'd sneer. "I told you that I tried that and it didn't work." Silence. That's pretty lame. Can't you do better than *that?*

"Perhaps you could order tickets in advance, which means that you would have made a commitment to attending."

She would curl her lip in disapproval. "I know myself. I would just be out the money. And I'd feel worse."

This would go on and by the end of the session I'd feel drained.

One time I feared that I had altogether slipped out of my role. As I said, Marta had a way of creating a pajama party atmosphere that made it tempting to let down my guard. At one appointment she was musing about some of her ideas for the future. It was a bright day for winter and the glare off her shiny silver belt buckle made me squint. She said, "I was actually thinking of getting an advanced degree in the psychological field, I don't know, maybe social work."

"Oh," I said. Sure. This made sense, given the kind of volunteer work she had been doing through a neighborhood church. She seemed to have a real affinity with young children. "You know not much more than a year ago I hadn't even thought of applying to grad school and — "

OH NO — SHE KNOWS HOW NEW I REALLY AM AT THIS!

I quickly brought the dialogue back to Marta and in a more useful direction. *Phew!* But I was horrified. How could I ever again have any stature in her eyes? What could I do to regain the proper distance?

The following day we were at our regular café — Tony was grading papers and Brendan was flirting with some undergraduates at a nearby table — when we ran into Nina. "How's the shrink business?" she asked.

"Not so good today." I told her that I had said something stupid in a session and then had trouble regaining composure.

"Oh," she replied. "A few days ago I heard an interview on NPR with some woman who's a therapist who was in a suicidal depression and through it all she was still seeing her patients." She chuckled. "In light of that if you're just getting thrown off a little from time to time I'm sure you're doing just fine."

Oh.

As though confessing my sins, in each instance I told Bonnie what happened as soon as I had the chance. "Try not to think of this as a therapeutic *failure*," she said at each juncture. "Think of this as a therapeutic *opportunity*."

As Bonnie helped me step back I saw that in fact these weren't utter disasters. Just as in a novel an incident may occur that doesn't seem to advance the plot but reveals another aspect of a main character, such situations give you information.

For instance, what happened with Marta confirmed what Bonnie and I already surmised — that she is very seductive. She pulls people in because that's how she knows how to relate to others and because she gets affirmation that way. "She is not going to feel any differently about you," Bonnie said. "You are still her therapist. Just keep going with the treatment."

As for Ellen, her response might have been defensive, a way of protecting herself from her strong feelings about not seeing me, Bonnie noted. Or I could have gotten a taste of how she often makes *other* people feel. I thought about how she frequently reports getting into tiffs with people and the disdain with which she describes her adversaries.

With Lucy, Bonnie affirmed my instinct that trying to gratify her every whim would not be productive. I said that this was difficult for me. My automatic response was always to *give* a client something.

"I understand that desire, but try to think of it this way: when you always try to meet a client's needs, you are not giving her a chance to grow," Bonnie said. "What you want to provide is *optimal frustration* — the client doesn't get everything she wants, and through this minor lapse she learns what she is able to do for herself."

Bonnie knew that I was struggling and tried to be supportive when she could. In her Winter Term evaluation she wrote:

"…This has been a stressful, intense, growth-producing quarter for Ms. XXXXX. Her capacity to experience feelings deeply has been both "a blessing and a curse." . . .In the same way her drive to immerse herself totally in the learning process has produced rapid professional growth, but has also created dilemmas and crises. Ms. XXXXX is truly in the process of transition, needing to master new roles in both her personal life, i.e. becoming a mother, and in her professional pursuits, ie. shifting her current career from being a journalist to becoming a therapist. [This situation has] created high demands and intensity of feelings."

"In the process of transition". Bonnie, too, was struggling to make my pitiful state part of a broader tale of personal and professional growth.

*   *   *

My appointments with Dr. Hammond were oases of lucidity. I felt so awful all the time that I was constantly struggling to get through the day. It was a relief to slump down on her couch and let the pain wash over me. I could then enjoy the release of tears. According to Self Psychology, the theoretical model that largely informed Dr. Hammond's approach, feeling understood is the adult equivalent of being held as an infant or young child. Feeling that someone was with me during this trying time, holding me in a sense, made it feel more manageable.

Once I noted that this nurtured feeling I was trying to make my own ran through many common childhood songs. "It's so basic," I said. "Isn't this the kind of thing we've been talking about all along?" I quoted from several songs Brendan and I had been singing along to:

Shoo fly, don't bother me,
Shoo fly, don't bother me,
Shoo fly, don't bother me,
For I belong to somebody!

Yes! *I belong to somebody.*

And, courtesy of Pete Seeger. ..

Somos el barco,
Somos el mar,
Yo navego en ti
Tu navegas en mi.

(We are the boat; we are the sea. I sail in you; you sail in me.)
   We are all intimately connected.
   And a little riff from a "Songs Around the World" tape that went:
   I'm little like a button
   And when we are apart

I put Daddy in my pocket

And Mommy in my heart.

I can feel connected to my loved ones without needing their constant physical presence.

Dr. Hammond nodded, cheering me on. "That's right. You're getting it."

"And all I need is to somehow get a grip on this idea, to *feel it* rather than just understanding it intellectually, and I'll be fine?"

"That's right," she said and shared a thought of her own. "You know, sometimes when I work with you I'm reminded of the children's book *The Runaway Bunny.* It's written by the same woman who wrote *Good Night Moon*, with the same artist. Wherever the bunny goes his mother is always there for him, up a mountain, in a sailboat. He keeps testing her and she's always there. I've had the sense that you've craved that always-there feeling yourself."

"*The Runaway Bunny,*" I said, sifting through my memories of picture books. "I don't know that one." I made a mental note to check the book out for Brendan, and myself.

I increasingly had the sense that this small suburban office was where the important things in my life were happening. It was this psychological journey that would help me feel better. I had always felt painfully disconnected from my own life. I was languishing on the margins. This work would allow me to move my chair closer to the table. And within this office I could feel safe.

The problem with the sessions was that they had an end. As we approached the end of the hour I would check the clock with increasing frequency, mentally calculating how much reassurance, sustenance or insight I would need in order to face the outside world and my own company again. When time was up I inevitably felt thrust out of my safe haven. But though desperate and out-of-control, I always played by the rules. I had to haul myself out of there; it was some other patient's hour.

I would stand in the doorway and ask one last, probably foolish, question so that I would have some phrase or idea to tide me over until the next session. I would then reluctantly leave the comforting dimness of the building and confront the glaring bustle of our small downtown center. It would take a moment for my eyes to adjust. It always felt too soon.

One odd aspect of my intense dependence on Dr. Hammond was that our lives were probably not that different. There were times when I mentioned a social or community event and she would smile in recognition as though perhaps she had also attended it with her kid (kids?) years back. She knew several people associated with my program. By her response to my literary and cultural references it seems we had been fed comparable intellectual diets. We were both married and mothers, with access to the same grocery stores, restaurants, and parks, subject to the same calendar and weather. How strange then that she had all this knowledge of how to function psychologically when I was living on the frayed edge of a breakdown.

I was not pleased with the dependence I felt. It wasn't comfortable. It wasn't convenient. It wasn't cheap. It didn't even make sense given the reality of my life. But alas such dependence was what occurred when you allowed yourself to regress and reexperience those crucial, primitive, early feelings. This was the price of health. No pain, no gain, as they say.

Already I was becoming less intellectualized and more immediate, Dr. Hammond pointed out to me. This meant that instead of taking several minutes to get into the psychotherapeutic groove I could launch into the day's topic fully immersed in the sensibility *du jour*. Rather than simply describing how I felt, I could recreate and *experience* that feeling. Basically this meant that in the therapeutic hour I had shed any remaining scraps of personal dignity. But what's a little dignity when I had *authenticity* and *cohesion* to look forward to?

Indeed, as I felt the barriers within me sliding away, I did feel that I related in a more direct way with others. I was more open. (Was this an illusion, or simply that my feelings were always at the surface?) So feeling bad was a positive sign, I understood. Learning to tolerate strong, often painful, emotions was important. After all, it wouldn't be like this forever.

And whenever I'd light upon something that felt true, some recollection of pain that rang with clarity, Dr. Hammond would be there with me, encouraging me to take pride in my courage and insight. By the time I found my way to Dr. Hammond, I had mined my memories pretty thoroughly. As in my own private literary oeuvre, I had built a wealth of scenes and images to allude to. A certain feeling state might evoke a particular memory. That memory, then, would lead back to the emotional world of a specific time. Through this kind of referencing and cross-referencing the raw material of my experience would at least appear to take on complexity. I may have thought I understood a given event before. Now I would see a new twist.

Here are the kinds of snippets of memory that would surface and resurface:

I was two or three years old and we were living in Yonkers, New York. My parents were out for the night (looking at new houses upstate? visiting grandmother Florence in the hospital?) and Mrs. Haigney was babysitting us. I kept coming out of the bedroom, begging to know when my parents would be home. I knew Mrs. Haigney was annoyed by my questions but I couldn't help it. I got up and asked again. It's dark; the door spreads shadow as I push it open. Now she is mad. "If I hear one more peep out of you...!" I return to bed, defeated and ashamed. Freddy is sleeping in his crib. He is no trouble. I am.

We were visiting the house we'd be moving to in Schenectady. So this was where my parents kept going! My father's shiny black Rambler was near the house and I watched my mother and Freddy drive up in her nearly-matching blue one. The roads were smooth, broad, and very black. There were few trees and very little grass. It felt empty. My parents needed to talk to the builders so I had to be quiet. I listened vaguely to the rumble of their talk while I played with a sewing toy: you thread string the width of shoelaces through the holes and made a picture, like a connect-the-dots.

I was stitching an elephant. I threw all my effort into the lacing until struck with the thought: "This is all well and good, but what happens when I finish this picture? *What then?*" The unscheduled future left me petrified. It was as though the instant I looked up from my play the world would end.

I'm twelve or so. Fred and I are standing in our dress clothes before a full-length mirror, about to attend some family function (a Bar Mitzvah? a party for some elderly relative?) "Does my hair look okay?" I ask. Hardly hearing me, Fred stretches out his arms and says, "I don't know. Are the sleeves of my jacket long enough?" "I think so. What about this color on me?"

We go on trading insecurities, dwelling in the same anxious, uncertain space.

One memory in particular seemed to speak to my ongoing emotional travails:

I'm five and at summer day camp at the local Jewish Community Center. At the end of the first week the parents are invited to visit. Our little group is walking from the main building down the pebbled path to the woods where the campsites are when I notice my mother and my next-door-neighbor, Beverly. Janice, Bev's daughter, who is my friend, rushes up and throws her arms around her mother.

I think, "I don't need to hug my mommy now. I'm a big girl at camp. I'll be seeing her later anyway." So instead of running up to her I give my mother a nonchalant wave of the hand. She smiles — okay, we're going to be casual about this — and demurely waves back to me. I'm proud of my cool detachment.

Moments later, I panic: HOW COULD I HAVE JUST LET HER GO! WHERE IS SHE? I absolutely had to see my mother *that instant*. The counselors could not stop my crying. I had to be taken back up the path, disrupting our group time, so that I could be reunited with my mother — who luckily was still in the building — for that hug.

That evening I was sitting in the bathtub and said to my mother, "I'm so embarrassed about what happened today."

"There's no reason to feel bad. You got upset and so you found me."

"No, you don't understand. I shouldn't have needed to see you. I'm really embarrassed. I don't think I'll ever stop being embarrassed about it. I should have just hugged you at the start like Janice."

"Don't worry," my mother said. "Someday you'll look back at what happened and laugh about it."

No, I thought. She will never understand.

Well thanks to psychotherapy I certainly looked back at what happened: backwards, sideways and upside-down. That one episode demonstrated my thwarted attempts at separation, my desperation to connect, and my sense of shame about it. Also, my shrinks and I deduced, this scene suggests that I got the message that it was better not to show feelings, even loving feelings. And it's a small example of what I did on a larger scale: held back or denied feelings so that by the time they came out they would virtually explode.

Once in a session, when the various threads of my emotional afflictions showed signs of weaving into coherence, when all of reality seemed to stand still in anticipation of some sublime balance, I said: "Boy this is intense. Maybe I will write about this someday."

Dr. Hammond smiled and replied: "I have no doubt that you will."

I must have been a gratifying client. I had such a long history of misery and such a vast range of complaints that any reasonable interpretation was bound to hit some chord. "You didn't feel safe." Sure, I could buy that. "You didn't feel special enough." Perhaps. "You felt like the "bad" one in the family." Now that you mention it. ...

For a long while we turned our attention to the pain of separation. Dr. Hammond noted that I sought help around the time that I had stopped breastfeeding, as Brendan started losing interest in nursing at about eight months. Hmmm... With Dr. Hammond's support, I worked through feelings about separation, grieving every leave-taking as though I was saying good-bye to that person — be it a shopkeeper or a friend — forever. I dredged up recollections of early separations (my mother giving birth to my brother? Being left with the scolding Mrs. Haigney?) and attempts to smooth them away (demanding attention from my father the minute he returned home from work — never a good idea.) I tried to teach myself to manage separations (*I've got Daddy in my pocket and Mommy in my heart.*)

At another point we discussed repressed anger, presumably a factor in chronic or short-term depression. I tried to deplete that invisible reservoir of rage. I punched my bed-pillows and practiced roaring like lions with Brendan on the living room floor.

Another focus was learning more about the tragedy of my grandmother, Florence. "Once something is known it becomes less scary," Dr. Hammond said. She urged me to get some details about this woman, not only about her illness but other aspects of her life: the circumstances of her arrival in this country; her difficult marriage to my grandfather, who my father describes as a brilliant but disappointed and resentful man; living in this country through the Holocaust knowing what was happening to her homeland in some now-desolate village in Russia. This added context would help me differentiate myself from her so that I wouldn't be haunted by the sense of there being a madwoman in the attic, a craziness in me that could erupt at any time.

To that end we tried to create a realistic picture of her. I knew so little. Most family stories I heard as a child concerned my mother's wealthy, eccentric family, the artists, writers, dilettantes, and dandies who came from Austria and Germany before the turn of the twentieth century. My father's side of the family (poor *shtetl* Jews) was much sketchier.

As for Florence, I knew the following: she was petite, about five-foot-one — my height — and a shade taller than my grandfather, Isadore. She used to cook traditional stews (to this day my father cannot abide the smell of stewed chicken, it so evokes the poverty of his childhood); she thought my mother wasn't good enough for her son ("too short,"); she called me, her first grandchild and the only one she knew beyond infancy, her "sunshine".

She also, my father said, had a strong rivalry with her younger sister, whom she thought was prettier. (Florence had a poor, highly reactive complexion, which I didn't inherit although my brother did.) And my Uncle Joe, my dad's younger brother, once said of her, "No matter what she was suffering, we always knew that she was looking out for us and thinking of us first." I have seen a few photographs: a short, matronly white-haired woman standing stiffly at the edge of a group at a family event.

With this my only data, this attempt to recreate my grandmother was a collaborative fiction-making exercise. Dr. Hammond and I built her up from scratch, a stoic woman of hidden strengths, haunted by personal and societal upheaval.

As I was putting my all into this treatment, I brought my writing into it. I liked the notion of linking emotional experience not only to the unconscious but also to my own work, which I figured was just another step removed. I might mention a line from an essay or story when it related to an event or expressed a mood. In one short story I had written a young woman lies awake in the middle of the night, listening to the sounds of the heating and plumbing in her family's house: "It always seemed that their house worked harder than other people's houses."

This opened up a line of inquiry. Why was the house working so hard? What did the family need protection from? Dr. Hammond would nod: ah yes, the family is working hard to clamp down uncomfortable feelings. Even the walls and beams seemed engaged in the effort. At the same time I'd think, "Hey, that's not a bad line," as I let the rhythm of familiar words settle about me.

Emotional states weren't just realized through my writing, but *reified*, literally made real for me. "That's it, that's it," I would think. "That's exactly what it was like." Only polished, worked-over work did the trick, however. I would periodically come across journals I had written in years past and threw them out. They were too painful to read and I didn't want them around. It wasn't that the material was so raw. Rather it was the self-conscious attempt to convince the invisible reader that everything was fine that I found so hard to bear. I did that at age 11 and 13 and 18 and in adopting the language of therapy, I was probably doing it now. Those amateur scribblings had to go. The author of them wasn't okay like she claimed. I knew better.

Above all Dr. Hammond and I worked to extend my range of emotions; it was crucial that I stretch my tolerance of intense feeling so that I wasn't totally bowled over by any strong sentiment that emerged.

She would sit with me as I breached my boundaries of psychological comfort: grief, rage, fear, elation. It was as if I were doing emotional calisthenics, working to flex those mysterious muscles.

I accepted whatever seemed like a plausible explanation for my problems. I was quite agreeable about letting my life be retrofitted in a way that made a given theory work. The narrative we crafted seemed to make sense; like my client Lucy, I sought order. Once we zeroed in on the cause, could the relief be far behind? You can tolerate a great deal when you believe it's in your best interest and you believe that you understand why.

I was also so unusually *well-prepared*. I knew the jargon. I could apply my powers of observation to my own case as well as to my clients'. I could take a nifty concept like "projective identification" and really run with it: "I've been carrying my father's sadness"; "I've been enacting my mother's fears." Such theorizing was reassuring. All I had to do was excise that one trouble spot and I'd be fine. And as for Dr. Hammond, who wouldn't be pleased by an acolyte who learned to speak her language with such devotion and dedication?

Dr. Hammond's theoretical orientation, Self Psychology, suited me just fine. According to this theory, developed primarily by Heinz Kohut, the task of psychotherapy was to address any deficits to the development of the Self. This was accomplished through certain forms of positive transference:

1) Mirroring (validating the client's feelings and experience)

2) Idealizing (offering a source of soothing and strength)

3) Twinship (helping the client experience closeness and commonality)

Some practitioners of this model describe psychotherapy as "applied developmental theory". This means that the clinician takes what she knows about normal development and employs that with individual clients, providing mirroring, idealizing, and twinship to jumpstart healthy development that had yet to occur. Pivotal encounters with important others — a parent, or in treatment, a therapist — are called, inelegantly, "self-selfobject experiences". A positive self-selfobject experience, as when a child feels understood by a parent, promotes healthy psychological development. (In a good self-selfobject moment you get an unmistakable *ding* of connection.) A negative self-selfobject experience, when the parent or caretaker responds in a neglectful, dismissive or derisive way, throws the growing psyche, the Self, off course.

Therapy in this vein involved constant affirmation with the goal of bolstering the Self. My Self and I were just *inundated* with positive regard. Every healthy step I took was cheered; every tear I spent consoled. I could revel in these emotional goodies and know that those gaps in my development were finally going to be restored. We were taking my skeletal Self, rickety and listless as at was, and buttressing it, like finding a broken mannequin in a dress shop and mending it, adjusting it for proper clothes.

✵   ✵   ✵

Since I had been handling my clients so well and the Agency had a growing waiting list I was given a new client, Lonnie. This made me a little nervous — my schedule was just beginning to feel manageable and I was wary of throwing off my balance — but I agreed to take her on.

This girl of seventeen was clearly from the other side of the tracks. My other clients at least had struggles I could understand. Hers were beyond the limits of my imagination. Lonnie's mother had left the family when she was a toddler, and her father had reluctantly taken her and her older sister in. She had a colorful, if rough, way of talking that at least gave me the comforting sense that she had an ironic appreciation of her circumstances. But these circumstances were not pretty. The family interactions were marked by beatings, threats of beatings, and put-downs so vulgar I blushed to hear them. She had once attempted suicide. The school she attended to try to better her lot was racked with violence. Also, she didn't look good. She was overweight and pimply, with the gray pallor of the addicted smoker. Though twice her age I felt a fresh flower beside her.

I had every intention of giving this client my best. During sessions I latched onto every detail that could possibly be construed as positive — her father suggests a pleasant outing, she gets some nice feedback from a teacher — probably to soothe myself as much as soothe her. I tried as well as I could to empathize. But on some level I sensed that too much fellow feeling wouldn't be a good idea. Even though she was my last client of the day and I was anxious to get home, I made sure to finish every last bit of paperwork concerning her case before I left. This way I wouldn't have the feeling of taking her story home with me, as if the sordid details of her world would sully my own precious family life. I was relieved when at one point she canceled three weeks in a row.

The Saturday following my return from spring vacation I was surprised to see Lonnie sitting in the waiting room a full two hours before her scheduled appointment. The receptionist caught my eye and mimed a shrug at me helplessly. Lonnie stood up when she saw me walk in. "You said you would see me now!" she insisted. I noticed that, unlike other times, she was wearing makeup, but it was applied haphazardly. She had painted on ghoulishly thin eyebrows and had bright red lipstick smeared about her mouth. She wasn't right. "I'm sorry," I said calmly. "There may have been a mix-up, but I do have another appointment scheduled for this time. I would, however, be able to see you at 11:00." That would be an hour before her scheduled session but still mean an hour wait.

"Well then, forget it! Leave it at noon!" she huffed, then grabbed her purse theatrically and stormed out the door. I had a queasy feeling about this exchange, but I was busy and attributed this unease to my own chronic anxiety.

I saw Marta, did paperwork during the eleven o'clock hour, and then Lonnie sailed in. It turned out that she was going to see a half-brother on her mother's side and was in a tizzy over it. I matter-of-factly suggested that something about this impending meeting was generating some anxiety for her, which she vehemently denied.

Lonnie went on ranting and raving something awful and I gave up trying to make sense of what she was saying. I simply put myself on automatic pilot and made a few noncommittal, vaguely soothing remarks. I was overwhelmed. I felt upended by her craziness. I wanted to get the hell out of there. I stole a glance at my watch, but the hour was young and time offered no sanctuary. She kept yelling and I kept nodding but was no longer listening. It was as though I had turned off my hearing apparatus, or was holding a telephone receiver, and the voice that was bellowing through it, far away from my ear.

At one point I caught sight of the window from the corner of my eye and had a fleeting fantasy of leaping out of it. I can now see this as expressing a quite sane desire to be out of that room by any means, a visual pun. But at the time, as distraught as I was over Lonnie's chaotic presentation, as biochemically confused as was my underlying state, I panicked. I was six floors up. My grandmother committed suicide by jumping out of a window! Was I doomed to the same fate? Was this some kind of fear or wish that was only now coming into consciousness? Was my inner world about to implode?

I made it through the session but afterwards I couldn't calm myself down. I got myself home, after unbearably long waits for the trains, but couldn't break free of the panic. If before I at least had some control over my own emotional thermostat now I had none whatsoever. I tried but couldn't quite convey to my husband the extent of my distress. It didn't make sense. I called Dr. Hammond and left a message. She called back with her dutiful, empathic promptness. We confirmed our Monday afternoon meeting and added an emergency session for Wednesday. I spent the next few days waiting for night and those nights waiting for day. I was calling Dr. Hammond an awful lot.

On Monday morning I told Bonnie what had happened and she felt terrible; this was one of the rare Saturdays that she was out of town. Usually she would be in the office seeing clients, offering me an encouraging nod or smile from time to time when we passed each other in the hall. She faulted herself for allowing me to be overburdened or not seeing that this new client was less well-structured (i.e. *crazier*) than she had originally thought.

"It's not your fault," I assured her. "I should have been more attuned to my own discomfort about taking the case."

We continued to dispute whose fault it was, but we did most definitely agree that Bonnie would take over Lonnie's case. We discussed exactly what I would say on the phone to Lonnie to make the transition as smooth as possible. I had to remind myself not to worry overly about Lonnie but to take care of myself.

Bonnie shook her head regretfully. "This seems to have been a very strong negative maternal transference. That can be very hard to take, particularly so early in one's training."

I wasn't quite sure what that meant and at that moment I didn't even care. All I knew was that I had blown an inner fuse and was now in a constant panic. The ground beneath me trembled. Every upper floor window I saw meant a potential, deadly fall; every spike of anxiety suggested damage I could potentially inflict or sustain.

Of all the disasters I had mentally rehearsed, I had not imagined that my clients' and my own stories could so disturbingly collide.

* * *

Despite waiting anxiously for three days I was a few minutes late for the appointment. For some reason all the street parking spaces were filled and I had to backtrack and park in a lot. Like I really needed this! I raced, breathless, to the waiting room, and Dr. Hammond stepped out a few seconds later to usher me in. I glanced at the digital clock on the ledge behind her chair to see what damage I had done to my precious fifty minutes. She waited for me to start.

"This was really, really awful," I said, my voice cracking on the word "awful".

"It certainly sounds like you were very uncomfortable," she said, clasping her arms around one knee. *Uncomfortable?* Must you speak in euphemism to me? I knew that trick (choose language to de-escalate the client's distress).

"Although now that I'm this much worse the background noise has stopped bothering me."

"Well that's something."

I was a mess. Moreover, our therapeutic *process* was a mess. With a barely disguised sense of defeat, Dr. Hammond suggested that I go to see a psychiatrist. A medical doctor. After having been cradled at the warm breast of the Lady Therapists for so long, this recommendation had the ominous tone of being sent up to the Big Guys. Did this mean that all the hard work we had been doing was for naught? Was I going to lose Dr. Hammond in addition to well as my sanity? Dr. Hammond assured me that the M.D. she was sending me to was a fellow she often worked with and whose approach she approved. And that she would fill him in about my case in advance. So at least I wasn't being thrust out of the fold.

Wednesday morning I took my customary El train downtown along the same improbable meandering route and nervously made my way to the assigned building in an elegant district on North Michigan Avenue. The elevator soared up to the 15th floor. Dr. Loftus presided over a fancy office on North Michigan Avenue full of chrome and up-to-date glossy magazines. I sat in the waiting room, overtaken with vertigo, and pretended to the other down-turned heads that I had the wherewithal to concentrate on *Conde Nast Traveler.*

Dr. Loftus was a youngish guy who dressed with the casual assurance of someone who thinks his time is worth hundreds of dollars an hour. He asked a lot of questions and revealed a not-unappealing wry quality as he listened to my responses. He was interested in the fact that I was in clinical training. He smiled warmly, even indulgently, as though thinking: "Oh young clinicians these days. Can't take the heat, can they?"

I heard myself describe my psychological history — punctuated by unpleasant details like periods of dizziness in childhood, anorexia in adolescence, psychosomatic pain in college, and long periods of sadness — and didn't like it a bit. If it were in any way possible I would have outright walked away from my own story and found one without all those dark corridors and blind cul-de-sacs.

It was as if in that moment I had stepped aside from my narrative and joined Dr. Loftus in dispassionate, clinical assessment, scratching chin and beard respectively. I said: "This doesn't sound very good, does it?" He gave me an arch, inscrutable look.

What should have happened: this was a perfect opportunity to make a paradigm shift, to interpret what I had experienced throughout my life as a pattern of psychiatric phenomena which should be treated as such.

What actually happened: Dr. Loftus made it clear that he had no intention of departing from the psychotherapy story line. He handed me a prescription for Xanax (for anxiety) and a prescription for Paxil (an antidepressant in the Prozac family) and told me the following:

1) This is your opportunity to work out all of this stuff once and for all.

2) Don't use the medication as a way to escape *your real problems.*

3) The relief you will get from the antidepressant will be subtle. Don't expect much of a difference.

4) If the antidepressant turns out to have any effect — and I should certainly be aware that there is no guarantee that it will — it will take at least three to six weeks before we even know it.

Then he turned to the topic he clearly really wanted to talk about. "With SSRIs, many people experience a decreased sexual response," he said. "But we have a whole bag of tricks to help with that." He gave me a prescription for an antihistamine. "This counteracts the physiological effect that inhibits sexual function. Just take this an hour before intercourse and I guarantee you won't have any complaints."

Huh? Believe me, sex was the last thing on my mind. And I should take this *an hour* before? I couldn't anticipate my mood *ten seconds* in advance.

Dr. Loftus was manifestly pleased with what he could offer me so I thanked him and added this last slip of paper to my ever-growing pile of prescriptions.

I was now informed that it was time for me to leave. "B-b-b-but," I said, trying to draw something beneficial from the exchange.

With the same wry smile Dr. Loftus held out his arms as though rocking a baby and swayed gently as if to say, "Easy, girl. We'll take care of you."

I gave Dr. Hammond a report later that day. Just as we thought, there was no escaping my story. I'd try a course of medication and perhaps it would moderate some of the pain of our therapy. It was then up to us to understand what happened during that nightmarish session with Lonnie and to find coherence in the feelings it aroused. We pushed up our sleeves and resigned ourselves to another round of long, slow work. We had a plan. I was relieved, and in my exhaustion almost giddy. I observed that Dr. Loftus's name would make a good name for an antidepressant and wondered if he had thought about trademarking it. "Or maybe that's just his stage name," I said. We laughed. I felt optimistic.

For that moment, anyway. My good moods lasted only as long as the thoughts they sailed on. That weekend we went to visit Tony's family. I was positively catatonic; we delayed our flight home because I felt I couldn't budge.

"I don't need you to be happy, Judy," Tony said, with understanding but firmness. "I just need your competence." I returned home, laden with bags of Tony's nephews' childhood toys for Brendan, yet more wobbly than before.

On Monday I dutifully came in for supervision but the minute I walked into Bonnie's office I felt myself crumble. I didn't want to be there. I didn't want to be anywhere. I looked around the room: an airless gray box. What was I doing there? Sitting on the chair seemed like too much work. Only the floor held any appeal to me, looked safe. So I lay down, flat-out on the beige industrial-grade carpeting that was every bit as stale and unyielding as it looked. And as soon as I did I began to cry: briny waves of tears.

Bonnie, whose presence I had scarcely noticed, spoke to me softly. "It's okay," she said. "It happens. I've seen it happen before." Her voice was a balm to me. I could feel it brush across my face, like a light breeze. "Sometimes one has to hit bottom before things start to come back together again. Just trust the process." Such understanding, such empathy, such depth, I thought as the tears eased. I wanted to lie there and soak it up forever. Oh, to be Bonnie's patient and not merely her student.

"Come on, now. Just get through the day now. It will get better. Just make sure you're in good treatment." She shook her head and muttered, half to herself, "I didn't like the sound of that downtown therapist you had before. I just know that she regressed you too fast."

Reluctantly, I got myself up and brushed the dust off my clothes. I still felt shaky, and more than a bit sheepish, but there was some relief: I guess I'm really letting myself feel the feelings, I thought. That could only be a good thing.

*   *   *

Amazingly enough the therapy sessions with my three remaining clients went smoothly. With Ellen I saw a noticeable shift. For several weeks she talked about a former colleague who had meant a lot to her but ultimately let her down. "Tammy meant everything to me, like a best friend," Ellen recalled. "Then, I don't know, she lost interest in me. I don't know, got busy. It showed me that I couldn't trust anyone but myself. And I don't." She tightened her jaw in a characteristic expression of indignation and hurt.

We discussed this friendship and I encouraged Ellen to explore what she had wanted from Tammy and what trust meant to her. She said that perhaps those things have changed since their friendship. In the course of this process she began to entrust me with new pieces of information, including some alarming details about her finances, and she began to lower her harsh facade.

Through our work Marta began to see that she could be more than the caretaker of everyone else's troubles. Because her mother had dumped so much on her over the years and because she so missed her father, Marta saw herself as the Queen of Sorrow. She told me that she collected little trinkets and beads in the shape of tears and kept them in a box beneath her bed.

Once she reported that she had spent the evening with Jeff, an old friend that she found appealing. "He's not my usual type at all," she said. "He's lively and likes to laugh. We even found going to the grocery store together fun. We ended up buying five different kinds of bubble gum and trying them all! I blew the biggest bubble — which of course ended up all over my face!"

"Isn't being fun a part of you, too?" I took the risk of suggesting.

"I don't know. . ."

"As you describe your evening I get a sense of your fun-loving side," I said. "And weren't you also a part of making the evening fun?"

She smiled. "I suppose."

With Lucy it was harder to tell. Sometimes she did seem more grounded. At such moments I became aware of her intelligence and could appreciate the career, social, and even artistic possibilities she would have once able to slow down and focus. Yet at other times she would pout or heedlessly fling her metaphor at me: "My room is a mess (*you* clean it up!)" It wasn't clear to me that her treatment was moving forward because there were so many stalemates. But Bonnie would consistently say, "You're doing fine work with Lucy. You're connecting with her in an important way."

Things took a new twist when one day Lucy mentioned a potential romantic interest. She had never before talked about men other than as pals. Sometimes we would talk about a friend of hers and it would be long into the conversation before I figured out he was a man, in part because they all had names like Sammy, Nicky, or Bobbie. This new man was a friend of a friend she met at a club. At the end of a long evening of chatting they had exchanged phone numbers and talked of getting together. As she described the encounter Lucy flipped back and forth between enchantment and disgust: "he's really tall/he's kind of gangly"; "he seems real smart/I think he's one of those egghead types."

When I reported about the session to Bonnie, she beamed. "That's a significant developmental step for Lucy, an Oedipal step," she said. "It suggests a shift in her relational orientation from the *dyad* to the *triad*." We therapists are such a romantic bunch, aren't we?

The culminating event of the internship year at the Agency was the Case Conference. Irving Kantor, MD, a venerable psychoanalyst of the old school, was a consultant to the Agency who led the entire staff in analyzing and conceptualizing cases that each clinician would select in turn. This was one of the educational functions of the Agency. Every Monday afternoon all staff therapists would trek up to the conference room and join Dr. Kantor in applying a Freud-tinted lens to a case that a colleague had prepared and we had all read in advance. With dismay I noted the many grammatical errors and inept word choices my clinical superiors made in their cases. How could these folks hope to salve the human spirit if they couldn't write a decent sentence?

Dr. Kantor was a sweet man with an endearingly dated quality to his speech. Women were "gals"; extramarital sex was "hanky-panky". He was like an emissary from a more leisurely time for a professional audience embroiled in managed care. He worked on the assumption that psychotherapy would go on forever. He might introduce a case from his own practice by saying, "In the first year or so we focused primarily on John's relationships."

I decided to present Lucy. I took this in part as a writing challenge. Could I write the case in a way that conveyed what it was like to be in Lucy's presence? Could I describe the vacillations between little girl ornery-ness and thoughtful maturity? Could the others understand why she frustrated me — and why I liked her?

I never really got an answer to my questions; during the conference we stuck to clinical basics, relying on the language of our profession and its strange, convoluted code. The result was an extended discussion of toilet training and earnest consideration of the diagnosis of Obsessive Compulsive Disorder. "That Filofax, that need for order, makes me think of OCD," someone said and several others voiced agreement. Then again, the person that made that suggestion always saw OCD, and the person who pointed out an Oedipal triangle always saw Oedipal triangles. In a strange way I felt my work with Lucy violated; everyone had a right to grab a piece of her story. It occurred to me that psychological diagnoses are not unlike horoscopes: they can be construed in such a way as to fit almost anyone.

Was the case presentation a success? Bonnie was pleased. She took copious notes during the consultation and from time to time I saw her nod in agreement. But I began to understand that many of the questions I was hoping to answer were not clinical questions but questions more of interest to a writer. I also wasn't sure whether anything I heard would be useful to the treatment. No one said anything that felt *true*. No one offered any suggestions of ways to help Lucy feel less disorganized that were more reasonable or promised more success than cleaning her bedroom or fixing her Filofax.

The parting gift for honoring my year of service to the Agency was a hardcover copy of Anna Freud's *The Ego and the Mechanisms of Defense* tied in a plaid ribbon. Then it was time to part with my clients.

Terminating treatment is a serious matter in psychotherapy. When handled well it can be an affirming, growth-producing experience for the client. If not it can re-traumatize her, stirring up feelings from unresolved separations or perceived abandonments in the past.

Bonnie and I devoted considerable time to devising termination strategies for each of my clients in accordance with where each was in her treatment and each person's particular vulnerabilities. Of course you can never predict exactly how someone will respond. Someone you may expect to struggle with it may use the situation as an opportunity to test out new strengths. Likewise, someone you thought would hardly be affected may unleash tremendous feeling at the very end. Bonnie pointed out that the relative resilience a client showed was a useful diagnostic sign. This information would then be passed along to the patient's succeeding therapist.

As it turned out I was greatly moved, and genuinely surprised, by this process.

Ellen showed admirable fortitude. She didn't get irate as I feared she might. Nor did she feign indifference. She openly said how useful I had been but rather than continue at the same Agency she went out and found an independent therapist that would be covered on her health plan. Calling people and being able to exercise her own choice gave her a boost of confidence. I had a phone conversation with the clinician she ultimately settled on and we were both stunned to realize we had something in common: both of us had been journalists before becoming psychotherapists — something that Ellen knew about neither of us. I reported this to Bonnie, who observed, her eyes a-twinkle, "Isn't it interesting how she found a way to replace you?"

With Marta the termination offered a chance for us to challenge how she typically handled relationships. When we discussed my leaving the Agency she kept bringing the conversation back to me. "I'm really happy for you," she said. "I hope you do really well where you're going next." As was frequently the case with Marta her first response was to take care of someone else regardless of what her own needs might be.

I said, "I appreciate your good wishes, Marta, but in this instance I would like to focus on what this means to *you*." She paused and mulled over this new idea. "Well, yeah, I am a bit disappointed. I like talking to you. I like how you say things. I feel like you 'get it', if you know what I mean. But you know, I still really do hope that you do well!"

Ultimately Marta felt confident that she could manage the change without pretending to feel nothing. She could also feel sad about our separation without infusing it with the high drama of a push-and-pull relationship. She could accept that we had been consistent with each other from the start. I reserved a spot for her at the Agency but she said she wanted to take a break from therapy while continuing with her medication checks.

I tread slowly with Lucy. When we first talked directly about her feelings concerning the end of our treatment, she rolled her eyes dismissively: Oh please, let's not go *there.*

I pulled her back to the topic. "I will miss working with you a great deal," I said. "I will wonder how you are doing." I talked a bit about the counseling center that would be my placement the next year to give her the "transitional object", tenuous as it was, of a visual image of me in the future — a potentially organizing principle at least.

She nodded, seeming to take it in. Her hair had grown out since her last confrontation with the razor and was now brush-length. She looked like a doe-eyed creature Disney might have created. Her Filofax was on the floor between us. I imagined Lucy, in that silence, projecting into the not-so-distant future when our Saturday meetings no longer served as a marker in the week, a time to reflect on her struggles, a chance to unfurl her confusions. I could sense her sadness in that moment, the most vivid expression of emotion I had seen in her.

Our final session was the hardest. How do you say good-bye to someone that you have been so intimate and at the same time so distant with?

As I had rehearsed in my mind several times beforehand, I said: "You and I are saying good-bye. And you will be moving on to something new. The clinician you are assigned to is a wonderful, experienced therapist." The man she'd be seeing had an excellent reputation; I had made sure of this. "He is just the person I would want for you. I know you will do well with him."

"Thanks, but I'm not so sure."

"I know." My throat clenched with that familiar desire to do something tangible for her. But there was no promise I could legitimately make. "No, your new therapist won't exactly replace me. You and I have our own relationship. But he will become important to you in a different way. He will challenge different aspects of you. I strongly believe that working with him will help you grow. I really do."

Then, in the final exchange of my first year of training, Lucy sat quietly, considering what I said, then looked straight at me and said, "I trust you."

YEAR TWO

I was glad that, unlike my clients, I didn't have to terminate my own treatment. I cleaved to Dr. Hammond as fiercely as ever, letting her provide stability through all the transitions I went through: between school year to summer, trainee to full-time mom, Bonnie's protegee to beginning clinician with my own knowledge and style. The spring flowers came out, school finished, the outdoor market opened — a major annual marker for people like us who planned our week around what we'd cook. Brendan said his first word (we think it was "teeth" but others followed soon enough.) And Dr. Hammond and I kept up our two-sessions-a-week pace.

I stayed on the Paxil for about two months. The mild side effects, like a slightly bad taste in my mouth and sweating at night (or could that have been the anger finally leeching out?), faded but I felt no improvement. I stopped taking it. Besides, if the *real* work lay in the therapy why bother with medication?

I have since learned: the 20 mg. dose Dr. Loftus prescribed is often not sufficient for a therapeutic response. Many people need 40 mg. or even 60 mg. before the drug kicks in.

Then there was the sex thing. I simply couldn't deal with Dr. Loftus's trick-antihistamine. I read an article in *The New York Times* about how some people took weekend "holidays" from their antidepressants to get around the sex problem and thought: this I can try. So on a bright Saturday afternoon, just as the Paxil was working its way out of my system, we took a family walk and Brendan fell asleep in the carriage. I looked at Tony and suggested we head home. We had walked some distance and had a limited window of opportunity.

Men often say that sex with a condom is like taking a shower in a raincoat. I will tell you that, at least for me, sex on a Paxil regimen was like taking a shower in a down jacket: all sensation muffled. But it was nice to feel close to normal again. Predictably, my weekend "holidays" grew longer and longer until they lasted the entire week.

Dr. Hammond and I forged ahead with our treatment. As for the medication she shrugged and said, "You really don't seem to me to be the depressed type anyway."

I found this pronouncement heartening, a vote in my favor. I also thought she was right. I wasn't exactly sad about things; I liked my life just fine. Nor did I lack for energy. Running around usually felt more comfortable than sitting still.

Our standing appointments — Monday and Thursday, Monday and Thursday — continued to be beacons of clarity in an otherwise chaotic time. At home with my family, whenever I relaxed into a pleasant sensation — warmth, tenderness, desire, shared amusement — my emotions would abruptly veer off in another, often frightening direction, as though there were tracks already set down and such twisted turns were built in.

Often these feelings were directed toward Brendan and Tony. I'd feel spikes of panicked rage together with a fleeting thought that I would hurt them. This scared me and I'd mull over these thoughts again and again in an effort to control them.

I was consumed by pyrotechnics in my head. Love so intense (warmth radiating from my breast) I couldn't bear it (*learn to tolerate strong feelings*). A vague, desperate greed-envy (I want-I want) pounding at my chest, like fear. Feelings slip from their moorings. Light turns dark, loving turns sinister.

"I don't seem to *metabolize* feelings very well," I told Dr. Hammond one day.

She dismissed my naive suggestion. All right, I thought. Silly me to put it that way. We then combed the content of the disturbing feelings that had emerged for possible meanings: rage, envy, vengeance, spite? If we could figure out what lay beneath we could defuse them. I was terrified by what I might uncover and regarded my own thoughts with nervous anticipation but I went along. I must be so close to a resolution, I thought. From my training I knew: the degree of the defense spoke to the magnitude of the need or injury. From that I concluded the greater the pain, the greater the promise of relief.

There were stretches when the pain and anxiety eased up and I might get a respite for several hours; there were times that I felt I was walking around with no skin. As the discomfort kept shifting in intensity and focus, Dr. Hammond and I could make the case to ourselves that the treatment was moving. After all, by this point we were both deeply invested in my recovery and this particular means of achieving it. So yes, we were still circulating among the same narrative details: my childhood illness, my envy of my brother and the fear that I had damaged him through my juvenile feelings, my grandmother's suicide, the imperfect parenting I received. From time to time I would experience a period of raw, sustained anguish followed by a respite of exhaustion and we believed I had made a breakthrough. Indeed, the pain, more than any other feeling, felt vivid, authentic, and real.

When things got really tough and I felt I needed to do *something* I would decide to try the Paxil again but it never did much.

"I wish there were a medication for terror," I once said to Dr. Hammond.

"Don't we all," she said rhetorically.

"Why are these feelings still here?"

"These are the feelings you need to work through in order to heal. They're in your unconscious, representing unconscious wishes."

Wishes? The dark envy of those I loved that I sometimes felt? Feelings of unbridled aggression? I was horrified. "But — but — " I managed to squeak out. "Doesn't that mean I'm an awful person underneath it all?"

"It's just your unconscious," she said, her tone implying *you should know that.* "Many people have such thoughts in their unconscious. Most don't have the courage to explore it."

Oh that's right, courage. How much courage did I have to have?

I spoke to her straight, not in patient-ese. "Dr. Hammond, this is the worst. You know I can handle almost anything as long as I have my love for my family to check back with. I'm losing my core." (That love for them is my center. Even you said that.)

"You'll find it again."

Thank God. "But where did it go?"

"It's still there."

"There's just this static interference we've got to clear out."

"That's right."

"Why do I have these awful feelings, in my unconscious, I mean?" (A drop as from the Torrey Pines cliffs; a mishap with a knife. A mental minefield; don't think that thought.) "It's something from my past. But what?"

Slight head tilt. An inquiring-open-supportive look.

"I don't know. My brother as a baby. I was jealous of him. I wanted to destroy him. But — "

"On an unconscious level, many mothers have some desire to destroy their child."

"Really?" (That's terrible.)

"On an unconscious level."

"Of course."

"Perhaps there is envy, or anger."

I strained for a memory that fit… "I wanted a baby so bad! I thought it would bring me happiness! And he did — but I also saw that I can't be happy. I can make him happy, but — "

Affirming nods.

"And Tony, when I love him so much but *he* can't make me happy. When I feel close but then I have this image of lashing out — " (The shadowy swipe of a sharp, feline claw.)

More nods. Emphatic.

"It's like I'm not ready for such closeness. Like I want to push away."

Silence: tell me more.

"It's all so confusing." All this shifting ground. I'm walking in the desert. I'm lost, thirsty, alone. The vista is endless. The sands shift with every step.

"We'll continue with this next time."

You're leaving me here, Dr. Hammond, in this wasteland.

She places her hands on her knees. She's ready to stand up, prepare herself to greet a new client. (Who I will walk past on my way out, avoiding eye contact, both of us. That's why magazines were invented, for waiting rooms.)

"Okay, I'll see you next time." We confirm the date and time. A ritual. Play the game.

Inwardly, I move a step away from my husband and son. For protection. (Mine? Theirs?) Just until I work this stuff out.

Sometimes I offered hints of what I was going through to friends, trying to feel out whether anyone else suffered from such feelings, but my sense of shame only bound me closer to Dr. Hammond. Only she knew the extent of my unconscious depravity and accepted me despite it. Only she could help set it right.

One Sunday afternoon I panicked while waiting for Tony and Brendan to join me in a grocery shop on our way back from an outing to the Lincoln Park Zoo. I reported this to Dr. Hammond and said, in weary disbelief, "I can't believe I'm going through these things."

She said, "Remember, it's not 'you' today who's feeling those things. Those are very old feelings of abandonment that you had as a young child and couldn't handle then that are now being worked through."

My misery didn't make sense to me. It was hard to accept that the basic elements of daily life were so daunting to me when others seemed to manage well enough. This made me grasp even more tenaciously to the idea that I *had to* fix myself. I held onto our therapy like a pit bull.

I wasn't alone in my frustration. Even Dr. Hammond's boundless positive regard faltered from time to time. "Sometimes," she said, with barely hidden exasperation, "I wonder if you are simply sitting in your pain. When painful material comes up you don't always have to go there. You can say to yourself, 'don't go there.'"

But it didn't work. I was inexorably pulled there despite all the willpower I could muster.

Our treatment went on full-force through the summer. I was still pretty wretched, but also somewhat lethargic and not a little bored. The focus of my days returned to the sidewalks, the lake, and the parks that were scattered throughout town. I put my professional clothes away in favor of shorts, a loose shirt, and sneakers. Brendan, now clad in those one-piece summer suits that are so sweet on one-to-two-year-olds, had become a high-speed crawler and I darted to and from conversations with neighbors and acquaintances to keep track of him. This constant starting and stopping of pleasantries left one hungry for more connection, which gave the impression that we had more to say to each other than we probably did.

I became friends with a poet named Dina. She liked a good walk, so she often joined Brendan and me on our treks from the library to the bookstore to the lake. We talked of writing and friends and families as we walked and stopped, giving me a chance to check Brendan's diaper or give him a kiss.

Dina lived downtown, in what was then one of the few high-rises around, so we sometimes stopped in for a break. I'd glance out the large-paned windows. From the ninth floor you could take in the lake and the trees and the homes that bordered it. This view was the pride of the place, but it slapped me with terror. We were so high up. Would I fall out? Would I be mysteriously compelled to jump? "You're okay, you're okay," I said to myself, standing in the narrow kitchen as Dina, oblivious to my irrational fright, poured iced tea. I'd be relieved when we the elevator delivered us to solid ground.

One afternoon I walked into Dr. Hammond's office and announced, "The id's up."

She laughed. "Ah. Let's hear about it."

I described what had happened. A while before I was wheeling Brendan around the playground and the crowd of kids running about — "big" kids compared to Brendan, four, five, six-year-olds — aroused in me a kind of dark, menacing feeling, as if something horrible was about to happen. "These must be old feelings provoked and evoked by the scene," I told her. "Childhood feelings." Always supportive of my associations, Dr. Hammond said, "You're probably right."

We then endeavored to open up id feelings: envy, rage, aggression, the darker hues of the mind's emotional palette. The effect was something like going tide-pooling at the ocean when there's a low or minus tide. Just as the water moves out, exposing usually concealed stretches of beach, defenses slip away. You peek under rocks and sift through sand. You climb onto a reef and find things you don't want to touch, even with your foot: curious treasures like barnacles; bits of disparate shell scraps, clung together; sea anemones — you poke one, it recoils.

These bits and impressions of feeling seemed to be steering us to an enshrouded but potentially intriguing piece of my past — when I had the mumps at 21 months. My father had once said to me, "At age two your personality changed. You were this bright, happy baby, and then, after you had the mumps, it was as though the world had become a frightening place for you."

I had dragged that memory around with me through all my various therapies. I had examined it straight, sideways, and upside down. Was this in fact my father's projection, and with his mother ailing and hospitalized at around this time the world had become a frightening place for *him*? Was there some trauma that I didn't know about? And now, with my own baby a few months into *his* second year, was my unconscious sending out a siren call so that I could protect him from whatever fate I had endured?

These were the kinds of thoughts that filled my mind as I strolled around town with Brendan. He and I were a team. I would sing to him when no one was around or quietly hum otherwise. When we stopped at a light I held his little hand. We used the stroller so much I wore out the plastic grips. Tony finished grading his papers and between stints of writing in his school office joined us on our happy travels. I bought tokens for the beach.

A few days after the emergence of the id, I was standing at the sink washing dishes and felt a jolt of nausea as though something had struck me from inside. "It was so awful! It was so awful!" I said aloud without knowing exactly what "it" was referring to, and started to cry. I turned off the tap, put down my sponge and gloves, and went to lie down on the bed to cry it out. (Soothing myself: two points.) Something in the particular character of this feeling made me relate it to that childhood illness.

I decided that getting some facts about this episode would help me make proper sense of it. I called home. My father answered. "What's up, Jude?"

I took a deep breath and said, "Hey Dad, I know this is going to sound like a funny question, but some stuff has come up in my, uh, therapy, and I wondered if you could tell me again about that time when I had the mumps?"

"You mean before you were two?"

"That's right."

Pause. *Oh, this must sound so stupid.* "Well, you had a very high fever, 106, and we were going to bring you to the hospital. But rather than do that, we chose to hydrate you at home. At that time this was done anally."

"What?"

"You heard what I said."

"How did I react?"

"You didn't like it. You screamed."

"I had no idea. It sounds really awful." I was already extending compassion to the hurt little girl that was me. "Did people really do that then?"

"Yes. It was very unpleasant but rather than bring you to the hospital and have to leave you there, we thought it was the right thing. But I often wondered, even later, whether that was best. I think it was too upsetting to you."

"Gosh." Earlier therapies had suggested that this time period was significant. Well, no wonder! But I had never really gotten to the depth of it before.

Now I thought, wow: a real life trauma. I was so proud — I found it. *Anal hydration*. How awful! And me, a sensitive child, probably already aware that my mother had caught the mumps too, from me. (Ah, that screen memory I had: my mother and I next to each other, propped up on pillows with bed trays, the sweet homey-ness of shared convalescence. Clearly a manufactured image to replace the terror of the reality, and the guilt — the sense of being punished for being bad.) This must be the crux of the matter, the reason for all my pain. Just like in all those books — *The White Hotel, The 50-Minute Hour* — a powerful cathartic moment after which all the pieces seem to fall together. Amazing.

I called Dr. Hammond. It was a Saturday, but how often does one have a true, Freudian-style abreaction anyway? She called back and when I told her what happened, commended my insight and fortitude. "We will work with this on Monday." *What a great therapist she is. What a wonderful patient I am.*

We worked with it on Monday, and Thursday, and a bit more on the phone while I was on vacation. Aside from the momentary rush of finding psychic treasure I felt no better. And so this great catharsis went the way of other psychological breakthroughs that led nowhere. We talked it dry then found some more promising material and moved on.

Perhaps my unconscious was speaking. But it's not clear what was being said. Maybe that I was a wretch. Or that I wanted to experience what I thought of as psychotherapy's Holy Grail.

*　*　*

Whenever I attempted to go back on the Paxil I would have my requisite meeting with Dr. Loftus. At different points I asked about the choice of medication. He would say, "Paxil is a perfectly good antidepressant." I would ask about the amount I was taking. He'd shrug. "It's a therapeutic dose. Why? Do you want more?" I would comment on the sexual side effects because, frankly, that was the only change I experienced.

Dr. Loftus's chief interest was: "What's happening in the therapy?" The medication and its potential effect were always a sideline.

I would mention a few highlights, careful to describe them dispassionately as though I were talking about another client and I was in control. "One question," I said once as if it were an afterthought. "Is it normal when you're going through stuff like this to have strange fears, like, if I'm high up in a building I have this feeling almost like I'm going to fall off?"

"It could happen."

"Oh. Okay."

What *was* happening in the therapy? A tweak of that old story, using the therapeutic relationship to change the plot lines. Dr. Hammond would demonstrate her refusal to abandon me by bearing with my pain and promptly returning phone calls when I called in a panic. She made it clear that she could tolerate the full range of my emotions, as unseemly as they appeared to me.

She encouraged me to feel compassion for the two-year-old child that I once was, that child that felt bad about herself, alone and unloved. This, she said, would help the healing occur. Together we commiserated with that young child, nearly weeping in sympathy over the unnecessary pain she endured. We would speak to her, back through the years, assure

84

her that it was safe to come out now, that indeed she was loveable and beloved. We would invite her back into the world, offering her a flashlight, a road map, the advantage of our hindsight. We would dress her up in the unconditional acceptance that only Dr. Hammond, with her clinical knowledge, empathic wisdom, and professional credentials could grant.

The vehicle for all of my work with Dr. Hammond was "the relationship", meaning *our* relationship. This edifice we created through our therapeutic encounters was a kind of freestanding structure independent of our lives. Dr. Hammond and I would continually take the measure of this relationship — its solidity, its permeability, its consistency — as an indicator of my mental health.

We talked at length about yearning, longing for the emotional goods. I had shown the power to bestow them on my clients, but I needed someone to provide them retroactively for me. Dr. Hammond performed this role, showering me with maternal care intended to solidify that tremulous core.

At the end of the summer we had to move. We had been renting the sunny top floor of a two-flat (a two-family house in Chicago-speak) and the landlord sold the house from under us. Most galling was the fact that the three graduate students who lived downstairs — who never shoveled the driveway and once let Brendan and his babysitter sit locked out for hours without so much as offering them something to drink — were allowed to stay because their lease was up later. Our friend Paul was taking a sabbatical year so we sublet his apartment, the first floor in a house he owned a block away. There was almost as much room, once we figured out how to safely transport to his office a fine specimen of a whale skeleton Paul had found and reassembled. We were lucky. But I knew I'd miss the brightness and graceful touches of our old apartment.

Our home was in chaos and I was pretty shaky when I started my next year's placement at the University's Counseling Center. Here I wasn't one clinician's chosen apprentice; I was part of a team of twelve trainees. Most of the others were more experienced. Many were Ph.D. or Psy.D. students. Some had completed extensive research projects. They freely used terms like "dual diagnosis" (referring to a client who suffers from alcoholism or drug addiction *and* a mental illness) and "anxiolytic" (a medication to treat anxiety). There was none of this "let's talk about empathy" stuff. Now the topics we discussed were our responsibilities in cases of threatened suicide or homicide and the fact that our clients were at the age where one's likely to experience a first psychotic break.

Nor was my supervisor a gentle soul like Bonnie with an inclination to coddle me. Rather, I was assigned to a very smart and efficient psychiatrist named Leslie. She was tall and slim and tended to wear power-type suits in bright colors. Nothing touchy-feely here. She might greet me by informing me how many Center clients she had admitted to the hospital or sharing a story about a student who had refused to take medication and then flipped out. She would react to a 3:00 AM emergency call the way another woman might to a broken nail. Her favorite clinical term was "decompensate". I decided that if I did no more than avoid embarrassing myself or my program in front of her I could call the year a success.

Our job at the Center was to serve as many clients as we could, and as quickly. As trainees we did lots of intakes. In one session we would meet a student and learn his or her trouble, take a history, and recommend a course of action. If a student needed to see a psychiatrist, or could benefit from one of the psychotherapy groups we offered, we would set that up. Students had a maximum of twelve individual psychotherapy sessions over their university career. We worked on a short-term model. When clients needed more or a different kind of treatment, we needed to refer them out. Only twelve sessions? That's barbaric, I thought. It went against everything I believed in.

* * *

Back in my own leisurely treatment we continued with my dreams. One dream that I still remembered had shaken me up a great deal when I was four:

A blue monster came into my bedroom. He was ordering me to do things. Although quite nervous, I remained calm enough to speak reasonably and say no to his demands. The blue monster told me to jump out the window. I said no. He didn't like that: I *dared* refuse him? "Jump out the window!" he said, louder this time. I shook my head, just as insistent. "I SAID, JUMP OUT OF THE WINDOW!" the monster shrieked, lunging toward me in all his huge and horrible blueness.

I snuck away from him, wandering down a long, curved path lined with knee-high plastic multi-colored flags like those flown near gas stations in those days. I walked carefully, furtively, checking back periodically to be sure that I had escaped the blue monster and then — WHAM!! — I bumped up against my bedroom door.

I burst into tears and flung myself on my parents' bed, telling them about my terrible dream and how frightened I was. I stayed in their room that night, snuggled in my mother's soft warmth. For years afterward I made sure to keep my bedroom door open at night. I was afraid that the blue monster would return. I needed a clear escape route so that I wouldn't be trapped.

How much had I known about what happened to my grandmother the year before? How much had my parents told me? What had I overheard? What kinds of fears and grief were unspoken? A full thirty years later, the questions prompted by this dream still seemed urgent.

Then there was a dream I had just after I began my first course of psychotherapy, my sophomore year in college. A disorienting feeling of dizziness similar to what I had had when I was eleven had come back and was troubling me. A suite-mate whose mom was a psychoanalyst suggested that I go to therapy. She gave me Dr. Gray's number and said that he's known for being a "tight-mouth" but he was an MD and an analyst and supposed to be good. He was a quiet, courteous man with an office in a residential area a brief walk from campus. I later learned that he had amassed quite a clientele among students and faculty through the years. I might be talking with another writer in New York only to realize that we shared this bit of history. "Ah, Dr. Gray," he or she would say with the fond bemusement he tended to evoke in his patients.

As the dream begins I am sitting in a conference room with several bearded men, clinicians of one type or another. Our voices are low, the tenor of earnest discussion. I am answering questions the best I can. The men occasionally break to deliberate over what I said. After a while one of the men rises and formally informs me that they have arrived at a judgment: they can now disclose what "my problem" is. I listen to their verdict, think "Wow! Now I understand everything!" and wake up. Their brilliant, illuminating conclusion, the key to my soul, vanishes.

I immediately fall back asleep and the dream continues. This time I'm in a small office with a female therapist. She's crisp and professional, with smart black high heels and an attractive suit, and is somewhere in her thirties. I am in my thirties too. We are having a friendly, animated conversation and again I am responding to questions. In my mind's background is the refrain: "I bet you never thought I had a weight problem." (I was overweight until age 14.) She asks questions and as I answer she records them on a board that she is holding away from me.

At one point she says, "I've got it!" and turns the board so I can see. There's a line of pictures and letters, a rebus puzzle. "I can't read it," I protest.

"But you have to — it's so clear! It's all right there!" she says.

"I don't understand the code," I say.

"Then perhaps you need me to help you," she says, and reads across the board slowly, her fingers pointing out the corresponding figures so that I can follow along. "There it is: "How can you do this to your brother?"

I wake up. *How can you do this to your brother?* I think, a sick feeling in my stomach. *What the hell does that mean?*

I used this dream as a touchstone through decades of therapy. What did the men say? What did this cryptic message mean? Why was it in code? What did the woman represent?

And kept finding new meanings. When I had my first female therapist: maybe the dream was telling me it was important for me to work with a woman. Perhaps the fact that the message was in code meant that I needed guidance in my quest for understanding. Dr.

Hammond and I noted that in the dream I had something of a peer relationship with the woman therapist. Maybe that was an indication that I would *become* a therapist myself.

Then there was that message: *How can you do this to your brother?* Again, that guilt I felt when Fred was born and had eye problems that may or may not have had something to do with my mother's case of mumps that she may or may not have caught from me. I envied this new baby, with all the attention he was getting, and acted out this jealousy in various two-year-old ways: I took a toy bat and hit a doll with it, saying, "This is Freddy." I told my mother to give Freddy back because I didn't like him. I peed under his crib.

I also perhaps *wished* bad things to happen to him. This was more psychologically insidious because, with a child's sense of omnipotence, I may have believed that any bad thoughts I had about my brother *had in fact* caused him harm. Maybe this was why my unconscious kept thinking I was bad. Maybe this was why I feared I would lose control and do damage to my son.

Dr. Hammond and I also continued parsing family relationships. Through the years my therapists and I had ferreted out the hidden pain my parents suffered from but could not face. "You are the healthiest person in your family," I was assured. "It's often the most psychologically healthy person, the one who is most aware of what's going on, who feels the most pain."

Then why couldn't I have been more messed up if it would have meant I wouldn't feel so bad? I wasn't above a little denial — if it worked. Fred, well, he seemed to be doing all right. He had become an art historian (yes, despite his eye problems) and was living in London with his family. But he wasn't actively grappling with all the family material — though he frequently served as a reality check for me, as I did for him — so he obviously wasn't as psychologically healthy as I was. Oh well, someone's got to sort all this stuff out, right?

In earlier therapies I was angry with my parents for not confronting their pain so that it showed up in my unconscious, as though it had been planted there and left to grow unchecked, like a weed. I'd fume, thinking about how their unconscious processes were doing violence to my poor beleaguered psyche. I thought they owed it to themselves and to me to deal with their feelings in a psychologically appropriate manner.

By this point I felt I was past that particular anger. But I gave Dr. Hammond an example from a few years' back of how my parents' inability to address pain affected me as an adult. Tony's father, Cecil, had died of a heart attack a few years before. He was a lovely man, a journalist who had moved to South Africa. Charming, if sometimes infuriating — there was no answer he couldn't question — he cultivated his eccentricities. His philosophy about money was: "I may not have enough money for the essentials, but I will always have enough for the luxuries." He wasn't young — almost 79 — but the family was stunned by the loss. (Although his widow, Liesel, in character, had the wherewithal to cook a chicken the day he died because she knew family would be arriving.)

Tony was deeply saddened, as were the many people Cecil had touched and, not insignificantly, amused. Over the phone I told my parents how hard the loss was for Tony. My mother said, "Why don't we come to visit?" We lived just north of New York City at that time, a few hours drive for them. "We'll cheer him up."

Well, "cheering up" is hardly what they did. Upon arrival my father asked, "How's Liesel?" but beyond that they didn't mention Cecil's death. Tony felt as if he was suffocating. "Is there something wrong with me?" he'd ask himself when he was unable to engage in conversation. My parents blithely went on, commenting on our apartment and other topics as though nothing of note had occurred in our lives. That night Tony told me he had never felt so alone.

The next morning I took my parents to a cozy, woody breakfast spot that served thick oatmeal and whole-grain pancakes. "I think Tony would really appreciate it if you talked more about Cecil," I said. "The fact that no one's talking about his loss, yet he feels so much pain, makes him feel awfully out of synch. I think he wants to know that you are with him and feel for what he's going through."

"Didn't I ask him how his mother was?" my father asked.

"Yes, but…" We talked more and my parents seemed to understand. They cared a lot about Tony and wanted to show that. We walked back and both my parents apologized and spoke directly about Cecil. "I'm sure this is a huge loss for you. He was such a wonderful man and so important to all of you," my mother said. I could see Tony's shoulders relax.

As this shows, my parents and I had found a way to deal with each other. I didn't endlessly browbeat them; they weren't rigidly defensive. The frustration I felt with them diminished with my growing understanding of my past. Dr. Hammond said that our improved relationship was a testament to the good work I was doing in therapy.

This pleased but also confounded me. Then why was I still sitting in a therapist's office talking about my parents? Before, when I could blame external forces — like my parents or my miscarriage — for my pain, the culprit was outside of me. I still felt bad but at least I felt I had some kind of integrity, some "me" that, though under assault, was on my side. Now that the pain seemed embedded within my being, I had no inner retreat. The pain was indistinguishable from myself.

* * *

As my work at the Center represented an externship rather than a practicum like the year prior, I spent three days a week there instead of two. This stretched the outer limits of my wardrobe, particularly during the long winter. I gave myself permission to wear a casual sweater as long as I paired it with a decorative scarf. I brought nice shoes and left my boots under the coat rack since, with space short, I would shift between several offices throughout the day.

Through intakes and assigned cases I met students from different schools within the university. I learned that each school was its own miniature society with its own rules and rhythms. And problems. There were undergraduates, with the predictable social and academic crises; the office always filled up after mid-term exams when many saw their grades slip. There were music students, journalism students, and engineers. I saw foreign graduate students trying to make sense of their surroundings, foreign students' spouses trying to connect.

From time to time I'd come upon clients from the business school. Sometimes they came in for a kind of psychological tune-up. As tuition-paying students they were entitled to their twelve sessions and wanted to get their money's worth. In other instances, the MBA students were seeking a diagnosis and treatment for Attention Deficit Disorder.

"What makes you think you have ADD?" I asked one tall, well-dressed woman about my age.

"I have trouble concentrating," she said, crossing her legs delicately. Her long fingernails were polished sheer pink. "I know I would be doing better in my classes if I got some medication."

As in a job interview, she had just described her excellent performance at the brokerage firm where she had worked for four years and noted that she had been accepted to every MBA program she had applied to. "How, then, would you explain how well you have done in school and work up to now?" I asked.

"I work hard," she protested. "I have to study a lot. Sometimes I have to read whole chapters twice in order to feel like I understand."

"Do you think that the work you're doing might be, well, hard?" I asked.

I did not refer her to any of our overextended psychiatrists. She was one unsatisfied customer.

The Center offered an interesting perspective on college. We clinicians saw the underside of campus life, the casualties of peer and academic pressure: the kids who were lost, lonely, or unequipped for life without mom and dad; the kids who couldn't handle the freedom; the kids who couldn't handle the rules. I'd sit in a spare office or the common room watching clinicians rush down the hall to receive a client or return a phone call, seeing all kinds of students bowing under the weight of their backpacks and their problems, and think about how a college counseling center would make a terrific setting for a popular television drama. Our bustling offices, the top floor of the college health service, had it all: tragic family stories from city and heartland; love lost and found; medical crises with quick, decisive action.

I didn't have the chance to develop relationships as I had with last year's clients. But I got into the groove of brief treatment and found I enjoyed the greater variety of cases. One student, Jake, was the first member of his family to go to college; he came from a farming town so small it barely made it onto most maps. He had come to school on a wrestling scholarship. Heavyweight, it must have been: he would lean back on his chair and his stretched-out legs reached clear across the room. We talked over his confusion about his role in his fraternity. "The guys think of me as a joker. I like to, you know, party and have a few beers in the evening. But I want to be taken seriously too," he said. I didn't see any joker here. He was warm and responsive, but had a sluggish way about him and spoke slowly and deliberately.

Leslie urged me to confront him directly about his drinking. She also suspected that he was depressed and asked me to give him a medical referral. "Drinking and depression are a deadly combination," she said. "We need to address the depression and he definitely needs to stop drinking." The combination of my supportive talking and, from behind-the-scenes, Leslie's cut-to-the-chase manner (she did put him on antidepressants) helped Jake feel better and more confident.

Then there was Michelle, a Southern minister's daughter. She had fallen in love with a student from Pakistan and was afraid her extremely conservative and racially-unenlightened parents would freak out. Michelle had the true gift of a story-teller and had a good yarn to spin; there were numerous plot complications involving her father's worsening Parkinson's disease, a sister being raped a few years back, and an ex-boyfriend whose uninvited attentions verged on stalking. With her down-home expressions and the leisurely cadence of her voice, Michelle always had me on the edge of my seat. I wondered if she was aware of the performance she gave each week, complete with the pacing of a good novel. I thought to myself that in going into molecular biology, she was wasting her gifts.

One case I was particularly pleased about was Eric, a chemistry student who came in because he was very, very shy. He was 21, a junior, and had never been on a date. He said he rarely talked to women, and when he did he would blush and want to hide. He wanted companionship, marriage, and a family, and knew he wouldn't have any of this if he sat home in his room every night.

Eric was sweet, even cute. He was slender and moved lightly. He had sandy hair parted on the side, nice even features, and a slightly vulnerable look. When he smiled one side of his mouth curled downward, as though showing amusement or happiness might be making too strong a statement. I could imagine lots of women having a crush on him. The trick was to get him out of his shell. We had just had an all-clinician pep talk on cognitive-behavioral therapy, which focuses on erroneous thoughts and maladaptive behaviors. What a great chance to try it out!

"Okay," I said, sounding a bit like a sports coach, "let's tackle this shyness." Has he always felt shy? Yes. What did it feel like to be shy? He felt he never had anything to say, and even if he wanted to say something he wouldn't know how. What does the anxiety feel like? Can we find some relaxation tools to calm it down? Can we try to look at social situations another way, less as a test of his status or appeal?

We went on in this mode for two sessions. As I was about to go into the third session I realized that I was dreading seeing Eric. I was feeling myself blush. The shyness was getting contagious. It had become this huge invisible creature sitting there with us, using up all the oxygen in the room. I knew I couldn't go through with another hour of aiming darts at Eric's shyness. It wasn't fair to him.

I sat down and took a deep breath while Eric looked at me expectantly. "We are going to shift gears today," I said, as though I had given the matter a great deal of forethought. "I just want to hear a bit more about you. About your life. About your family. About anything. Just about you."

"Really?" he said, taken aback. "Like what?"

"Okay, tell me how your family came to live in Chicago."

He was tentative at first and then the words started to flow. He told me how his mother's parents came over from Czechoslovakia and how, after failing at farming, they opened a small grocery store west of the city. Did he remember them? Did they tell him stories? Eric seemed surprised at my interest but as he went on he embellished his narrative with details and his own insights. It occurred to me that I was essentially modeling for him the kind of conversation he rarely got to have — especially with women — a conversation marked by interest, curiosity, and mutuality. I could see him winning himself over with his own tale. At the end of the hour I asked him how he felt about the session. "Good, I guess," he said, back to blushing. "I didn't know I had so much to say."

"Or how interested someone else might be in what you had to say."

"Right."

We continued like this for the next few sessions. He seemed more relaxed and confident. He said that in class he sat next to a girl he found pretty. He was about to talk to her — and would have ventured something had the professor not started talking first.

At one point I said, "I think that what's happening is that we're beginning to look at your situation in a new way." I drew two circles. "Before, you had this problem, your shyness, and we were trying to get rid of that problem." I drew arrows across one circle. "Now, we can see that you're this multi-dimensional person, with many aspects and attributes, and shyness is just one small part of who you are." I drew a pie chart, with one narrow sliver representing shyness. "That in itself doesn't define you."

In our last session, we talked about how Eric could apply what we talked about. He said he already had his eye on a young woman, also a student, who would be working at the same lab over the summer. I suggested ways to find out fun events happening in town. Though an avid golfer, he didn't know there was a community course near campus. As it was time to say good-bye, he held my gaze without blushing and said that the treatment was far more valuable than he had imagined it would be.

I proudly reported this case to my masters level supervision group. "I'm kind of getting it now," I said, excited. "Brief therapy is kind of like a short story — you carry through one theme and work toward a single epiphany. *Long-term therapy* is more like a novel. You get the whole picture, not just one perspective on it, and work with lots of interconnected themes." Henry, the senior clinician at the Center who was my small-group supervisor, nodded. "That's right," he said. "You could see it that way."

These bright successes were not, unfortunately, reflected in my own mood. As we moved through the winter, I started feeling worse. Because of Leslie's work demands I didn't always know when she and I would meet for supervision. When she had a spare hour and invited me in, I often felt like a wreck. Rather than the openness I had with Bonnie, I was on guard. What if Leslie knew what a mess I really was, I wondered. Would she still trust me with my clients? In the middle of our meeting Leslie would invariably get a phone call about some extreme case, as was her specialty, and I would sit there, consciously unobtrusive, staring at the jar of jelly beans on her desk. I feared that if I let my eyes stray, they would light upon a book about some disorder that I would then fear I had. I wished I could sneak out of the office, barricade myself in some spare office, put down my head and cry. When Leslie got off the phone and we resumed talking I was always surprised by how controlled and articulate I sounded. It was an act of sheer will.

All clinicians at the Center attended disposition meetings, where we would go over the intakes of the week and assign cases to clinicians. As the winter term got underway the stack of forms and files to deal with grew bigger and bigger. That middle trimester was a killer for everyone. Days were short. Chicago winters were long. There were few breaks allowing students to catch up on their work. We were doubled up in offices and worried about having enough space to see clients. The cases were more desperate now. Students who had thought they could put off dealing with their problems were realizing they couldn't.

By now we could only get through the meetings with a dose of gallows humor. "Pamela, you haven't had any suicide cases this week. I think you're due." One by one, Al, our team leader, would read over the files. "This client has been seen here before," he'd say. "This requires a senior clinician." I'd hear pages flipping as a half a dozen people in the room scoured their calendars in search of open space. "I'm really at my maximum," one would say. "I could do it, but only on a Tuesday afternoon," another offered. Someone always made room in their schedule. We took our jobs very seriously. We were, after all, the bulwarks of emotional stability on campus.

Al would read enough details from the intake form to give a sense of the case and what was required. Such awful things these young kids were dealing with: losing parents in accidents; siblings suffering from terrible illnesses or on drugs; eating disorders; physical abuse; poverty; rapes. What was the meaning of all this suffering? What was the *point*? I would berate myself for being depressed and edgy when I didn't have anything terrible to complain about. At the same time, I would hear these horrors and empathize so deeply it nearly felt they were all happening to me. My psychological boundaries had grown more porous. I tried desperately to maintain an air of clinical detachment.

Since so many first-year students were coming in with similar adjustment problems, a senior clinician named Darlene and I decided to start a freshmen group, meeting every Wednesday afternoon. I liked Darlene. A thirty-year veteran of the Center, she had a soothing, grandmotherly manner. Her clinical specialty was grief.

On those long winter Wednesdays, smack in the middle of those long winter weeks, I'd set up for the group, dragging five or six extra chairs into Darlene's office. The sky would already be growing dark. One by one the students came in, wriggled out of bulky coats and backpacks, and sat down. I smiled reassuringly at each one; such a pillar of mature adulthood I was. Out of the corner of my eye I'd see our reflections appear in the window. The shapes of trees and buildings, reminders that I was part of a larger world, disappeared with the day's light. I felt closed in the room amid the dark, closed into myself among the group.

Darlene and I encouraged the students to talk about their feelings and frustrations. "Does anybody else besides Ginny feel that students are overly cliquey here?" I might ask. "Has anyone found a way to successfully get around that?" I'd nod solicitously at each response. Darlene and I would weave their stories together, arrive at commonalities, help the students make sense of their collective experience. Privately I counted the minutes until the group ended, knowing full well that once it did I would once again be at a loss as to what to do with myself.

After each session Darlene, in her nurturing, attentive way, asked, "How do you think the group went today?"

"Well," I would say, weary after a full day of processing feelings and experiences, wanting simply to leave, "I think it was a good session."

"I do too," she'd confide as we moved the chairs, dismantling our friendly circle.

I was feeling worse and worse. Social events that, however temporarily, would normally take me out of myself, were excruciating. I had become so fragile that I could tell Dr. Hammond that I got through the day without unraveling or was able to make small talk with someone and she would applaud me. "Very good," she would say as though I were a child.

The depth of my anguish and disorientation was getting harder to express in words. "Try to think visually," Dr. Hammond said. "If there's a picture in your mind, what might you see?"

I closed my eyes and thought for a moment. "I see myself walking and falling into a hole."

"What does the hole look like? What is around it?"

"It's dark and deep and bigger than a manhole," I said. "There's a pole next to it, something I could grab onto to pull myself up."

"There's something you can grab onto," Dr. Hammond repeated. "Remember that."

One Saturday Tony and I had a dinner party: ten people, three curries. Dina and her husband, Steve, were there, Nina and her boyfriend, two other couples. I had been up all night, mired in dialogue with my own wretchedness. We had a busy day cooking, cleaning and setting up, and sooner than seemed possible our guests arrived. I was a shaky mess. How could I handle this? In the kitchen, I cornered my friend Lori. "I didn't sleep at all last night," I said, my voice wavering. "Have you, have you ever — " Goodness, how could I even begin to explain this? "Have you *ever had a bad night?*"

Lori took my cue and responded with sympathy. "Oh, Judy!" she said. "You're so hard on yourself! I am the queen of the white night. Everyone here, all your friends, have faced and thought about tough things. That's why we're here. That's why we're your friends." She gave me a big hug.

I felt embraced by friendship itself. Oh, such great people. What would I do without my friends?

One day in late winter I felt particularly bad. A deep gloom had settled over me. It was socked in, like a fog. A line from one of Emily Dickinson's poems kept running through my mind: "*This is the hour of lead.*" I had a little time between clients around lunchtime and I wandered over to the local Borders. I saw Dina. Normally I would go over immediately to say hello and chat, glad for our serendipitous meeting. But now I was hoping she didn't see me. I didn't want to talk to anyone. I wanted to be invisible.

Dina did see me and gave a friendly hi. My response must have been odd. "Are you okay?" she asked.

"Sure, I'm okay."

"Are you *sure?*"

That night was really bad. Aside from being up all night, which was becoming the norm, I was roiled by dark feelings. I couldn't feel love without feeling hate. Tenderness turned to feelings of aggression that didn't seem part of me. They scared me, like a threat of physical assault. These feelings were random and aimless, like little shocks of rage, but as

I was cuddled so close to my family it seemed to soil my very love for them. I was alone but for these inchoate emotional sensations, which seemed to have always been there and seemed that they always would be. Would they finally overtake me altogether, pulling me down with the dismal gravity of lead?

Brendan (who was in our bed) gave a hearty grunt. I turned over and moved my pillow in response, a hopeful gesture in that there was even a remote possibility of sleep. But it made no difference whether I lay on my back, side or belly.

I had an overwhelming sensation of nausea but this physical feeling was somehow contained in my head. I had this horrible feeling of my head about to explode. I hated what I was feeling. I hated myself. I was terrible and worthless. I wanted to die. Anything to stop that feeling. Oddly, thinking about dying gave me a bit of a respite from the pain, a perverse form of detachment.

I went to my regular Thursday morning session with Dr. Hammond at 9:00. It was a cold gray day. As I got out of my car I looked up and saw geese flying, making their way back for spring. "Oh, they're so beautiful," I thought tearfully, seeing the birds as soaring, squawking signs of hope. If there's beauty, there's hope... Still, as I went inside, it felt like the end of a very long day rather than the beginning of a new one. Even the sanctuary of Dr. Hammond's office felt airless and dark; I couldn't quite hold on to that sensation of mind taking wing.

I told her how awful I felt. "I think I should go to the hospital or something," I said. "I just can't take it anymore."

She looked concerned, even a little pale. "Before we do anything like that let's try to understand what's going on," she said calmly. "I am not seeing someone who's ill. I see someone who's in terrible pain. Let's try to understand that pain."

In a choked-up voice, I told her about the geese. "I felt thankful to see them," I said. "Maybe the flip side of the pain is thankfulness, a feeling of gratitude for the beauty of nature and for everything I have." When I saw her nodding eagerly I knew I was on the right track.

I cried and talked, cried and talked the whole hour. We comprehended the night's pain as the sadness that the feeling of childhood grandiosity was trying to hide, an intolerable vulnerability and fear. "Whatever you're feeling now you've felt before, at some point in your life — and survived," she said. "Let that be a source of encouragement." Dr. Hammond was so gentle, so understanding. I was so lucky to have her. I was teeming with thankfulness. By the time I left the session I felt not just lighter, but exalted.

That day I took Brendan to a children's museum. I watched him clamber over the large wooden boat. I carried him through the rooms for older kids and found buttons for him to press. I was bursting with love for him. I was bursting with love for any child I saw. I smiled at other mothers, several of which looked as tired as I probably did. Oh, we all have our struggles, but underneath we all want and need the same things. I had this sense of dewy freshness; the whole world around me was new. We lingered about until Brendan got restless and I took him home for lunch and a nap.

Nap — that was a concept.

I went on the Paxil again. I learned that whenever I felt anxious or awful I could bring those feelings back to that core sadness, reeling my feelings in so that they didn't seem so overwhelming. In time, Dr. Hammond said, I would work through that sadness and not have to feel it so intensely. This made sense to me. So I had hit bottom and survived; everything was going to be okay after all. I did start to feel a tiny bit better, still melancholy but the idea that it would soon lift sustained me. Was it the Paxil? Was it our work? The improvement was so subtle that I couldn't imagine that it had anything to do with the medicine. I had just experienced a huge psychological metamorphosis, hadn't I? I went off the drug again. With my appointments with Dr. Hammond to hold onto, I had the feeling of pulling myself slowly but surely out of a deep hole.

A few weeks up from the low point my parents came to visit. My mother and I sat on the living room floor, playing with Brendan. I had just bought *The Rainbow Fish* and he was pointing at the shimmery spots. I glanced over at my mother: never too good or too grown-up to get down on the floor with a child. I was flooded with loving camaraderie. "Mom," I said tentatively as Brendan's attention turned away from the book back to Tony. "I've been going through a tough time." She looked at me attentively. I tried to put into words the bittersweet ache I was just barely able to keep under control. "Well, I've been in therapy again, you know, and it's been quite intense, and I've been going through some very painful material, and — "

She looked at me with affectionate resignation. "You put yourself through a lot, don't you, Judy?"

While all this was going on, Tony and I were confronting the disconcerting reality that we had no set income for the coming year. Tony's teaching job was what's known as a "terminal position", meaning three years and that's it. Faculty members in several departments, English, Creative Writing, and African Studies, were trying to extend the appointment but the best the school could come up with was two-thirds time at two-thirds pay. Where would we live? Would we extend our sublet another year? Paul needed to know. How were we going to make a living? I had no specific prospects (I figured I'd start job hunting in the summer) and had let my writing work dwindle to nothing. I was so bound up in my own agony, however, that I let Tony do most of the worrying.

Then he got interest from Bennington College in Southern Vermont. He went out for an interview and liked the faculty and students he met. An offer came in. I heard about the negotiations while talking to Tony from the Center staff common room, with busy therapists streaming in and out. Maybe we'd be moving back to the East Coast. I didn't realize how much I wanted to do that until the possibility presented itself.

While I was more comfortable with the routine at the Center, I was becoming frustrated with the clinical work. Clients came and went so fast. As spring vacation yielded to exam time, which would then lead into summer, students switched gears so quickly it was hard to know what was really going on with anyone, or what they really needed from me. Much of the magic of the previous year — the unspoken communication, the listening beneath the material — wasn't happening in the same way.

As my role was often to get information from new clients, it felt more adversarial. Rather than trying to get a visceral sense of what someone was experiencing, I often thought, "Is this person lying to me about how much he's drinking?" or, "When she says that she used to be bulimic but 'doesn't do that anymore' do I take this at face value, or refer her for some medical tests that might reveal if she's still bingeing and purging?" I knew that our mandate was different here, but I wondered whether I was losing something important about the therapeutic process. It occurred to me that I hadn't heard anyone utter the phrase that had been Bonnie's mantra: "Listen to the client."

At the end of the year Leslie gave me my performance review. She closed the door and programmed the phone to bounce to the receptionist; no emergencies would intrude. "I don't know what you write but I can see that you have the sensibility," she said. "You have the kind of gift in this line of work that can help people lead richer lives. I don't see you doing in-the-trenches kind of stuff, or dealing with difficult cases. You're too sensitive to handle that. It wouldn't be good for you. It also wouldn't make use of your strengths." She had given more thought to my work than I had imagined. She seemed to respect me more than I imagined, too.

"Where do I go from here?" I asked.

Get more training," she said. "Get your license. Get lots of different experiences. This work is all about experience, and finding good people to work from. Develop that sensibility of yours. You've got something. Find opportunities to do more long-term work. I can see you struggling with the brief method."

This confirmed my feeling lonely in my orientation. But where to go? What would I find on the East Coast? I had thought that my degree would land me somewhere. I felt too old to merely have potential.

Late in the summer we made our move to Vermont. As things were in a calmer phase in our treatment — a twice-a-week therapy phase as opposed to the three times crisis mode — Dr. Hammond and I wrapped up the package and pronounced me healed. As well-versed as I was in the tenets of therapy, I knew how to respond so as to appear sound. I knew all the right answers. And when I wanted to — such as when I was about to pick up and move a good thousand miles away — and was busy with real-world tasks, I could shift those to the foreground and put the pain, worry, and other assorted symptoms in abeyance.

This meant abruptly changing direction in our therapy as we devoted our final last six weeks to grieving the impending separation. Every time I sank into pain or sadness I could say, "Oh, that's the grief," and everything made sense. I remembered that the teacher in my training class had said, "The more successful the treatment, the more intense the termination would be."

Dr. Hammond and I worked diligently, examining that grief from every angle and within every niche. We grieved absolutely everything that could possibly be grieved in an attempt to work out my ample feelings of unresolved grief. Yes, this fugitive grief must be what has been holding me back. This unexpected change in my life presented a chance to disentangle all those old feelings. Oh, how convenient. Isn't it wonderful how life gives us an opportunity to address the unconscious?

Two days before our move, Dr. Hammond and I shared a nice, appropriately poignant termination, recapping some the highlights of our work together and congratulating ourselves for working through them so effectively. I had my Masters in Counseling Psychology, and ending treatment with Dr. Hammond felt like another kind of graduation.

YEAR THREE

I immediately fell in love with our quirky little corner of New England. It reawakened a visual appetite after four years of looking at the flat horizon of the Midwest. The town and its surrounding areas were a lot like the landscape of my childhood, an hour due west in upstate New York, but had the backdrop of these glorious mountains, constant but ever-changing, always playing tricks with the light.

How do you explain an elemental connection with a landscape? How do you quantify visual happiness? From talking to others I quickly learned that rural life wasn't for everyone, but something in me knew that I wanted to make a go of this place. The friendliness and small-town coziness made me feel welcome. Everything was more affordable. Rent on our red farmhouse in the campus orchard was less than half what we paid in Chicagoland. The scale of community life made everything I would want to do seem possible. Blueberries to pick. Or apples. An organic goat farm where Brendan and I could wander. A waterfall, thunderous with its force, a short walk away. With Brendan tucked in his car seat behind me and a map by my side, I maneuvered my way around local country roads and thought: I can't believe I am surrounded by so much natural charm. The chance to enjoy this every day felt like a gift.

Brendan was now two-and-a-half, and rural Vermont gave him lots of running room. Tony and I would marvel at the astonishingly beautiful sight of Brendan frolicking, a bright bundle of pleasure and curiosity, about the fields nearby, fields that would soon be covered with leaves and then snow. There was a fine preschool for him. Because numbers in Vermont are virtually by definition small, he was receiving the close adult attention that he thrived under. He developed a passion for keys and became a minor celebrity on campus for asking to examine everyone's keys. He carried keys around with him all day. A transitional object, I noted. Is my son together, or what?

Tony was busy with work and I intended to find a clinical placement and work towards my therapist's license. I was already picturing a quaint renovated farmhouse with the barn converted into an office for my (thriving of course) private practice. Or a sun-filled contemporary post-and-beam, with a room set aside for seeing clients. I would be wearing casually chic clothes, certainly in natural fibers, probably earth tones. "Yes, come on in," I envisioned myself saying to a client, leading him or her into my bright country home, the scent of fresh-cut flowers and baking bread suffusing the background. I made phone calls and set up a few meetings. I put my graduate school papers into professional-looking black binders.

Through September and early October, our legendary foliage season, we were outdoors constantly. People were always around, happy to introduce themselves and chat. Brendan's sense of wonder was contagious; the beautiful but slightly scruffy landscape literally begged one to play. Brendan liked, with help, to walk on logs or planks like a balance beam, something he associated with performing in a circus. One day he was disappointed because a favorite log was no longer there. It was late afternoon; the shadows were low and long. I noticed the shadow of a tall tree that stretched all the way across the lawn and amused Brendan by walking that shadow, holding my arms out for balance so that I didn't fall. He squealed with delight and asked for a turn. We played on our pretend log, the one lent us by daylight, until the darkening sky told us it was time to make supper.

It was the balmiest, most colorful foliage season in years. "Don't draw any conclusions from this wonderful weather," warned Hilary, another woman dragged here by her professor husband and who lived across the orchard. "Fall isn't always like this." Indeed, it started getting colder. I had been so busy at first, so pleasantly, even euphorically, distracted by novelty. Then I was spending more time in the house. My mood would slip up (into anxiety) or slip down (into gloom). Hold it, I would instruct myself. Tread that mental balance beam. Try to make use of all that I learned in therapy.

At the end of October we set the clocks back. It got dark outside earlier. I put the lights on earlier and in greater force. I would ply my will, trying to push back the darkness creeping in.

I was increasingly shaky. I would go along, conscious of momentary happiness, and then my mind would take a sharp curve, like a car swerving with screeching wheels at high speed. To wit: I'd be walking in the woods, crunching leaves with each step, enjoying that satisfying sensation and the crackling sound. And think: isn't this lovely? Ah yes. Vermont is so quaint with its changing seasons... Then I'd be sideswiped by a completely antithetical, utterly horrifying thought: what if all this is meaningless and life isn't worth living after all? Oh no. My grandmother committed suicide. What if something terrible like that happened to me? (As if suicide were something that just happened to one.) *What if!*

This was not good. The discrepancy between what I thought (I was blessed) and what I felt (this was hell) became untenable. Not knowing what else to do, I called Dr. Hammond. "I'm having trouble managing affect," I told her in a small voice when she returned my call.

We assumed this was a minor upset. We discussed the joy I was feeling in this place and how that was new and possibly frightening in its newness. Then we started doing therapy on the telephone. Perhaps there was just a bit more work to be done, we rationalized, you know, just smoothing out the edges. For me to find and begin work with a new therapist here would be such an ordeal. Certainly after the robust therapeutic relationship Dr. Hammond and I had worked so hard to form.

A part of me thrilled to this reconnection. We were back in our therapy, back to the intimate shorthand we had created for how I experienced the world. I could also reclaim the promise of psychological overhaul, the brass ring of transcendence. There is something very seductive about the belief that you will feel better, and something quite gratifying in the notion that the vehicle for improvement is your own effort.

So back to work we went. As each scheduled session approached I would take the phone into the spare bedroom I used for my office and close the door though no one else was home. I wanted to approximate the experience of sitting in her office as much as possible, despite the fact that rather than an airshaft I was looking out over a walled garden and an old red barn used for storage. Over the phone we attempted a kind of metaphorical transplant. Dr. Hammond would offer the trust and well-being that was eluding me and we would try implanting it in my psyche. She would provide warmth and affirmation and I would try to assimilate it.

This was, incidentally, a process Brendan and I engaged in every day when I brought him to preschool. I would give him a big hug and then go outside and blow him a kiss through the window. He took that kiss and put it in his pocket. And have it with him all morning.

But with me it wouldn't take. I tried to be creative about it. Inspired by Brendan and our kiss, I tried carrying a quarter in my pocket and telling myself that it represented Dr. Hammond's care and concern. My transitional object. It did nothing, not even twenty-five cents worth. How infuriating it was to understand concepts like object constancy, transitional object, and separation, and be able to discuss them in theoretical terms, and yet not be able to perform such an elementary task myself.

"You can give up the pain," Dr. Hammond would say. "You can make the decision to do so."

"No, I can't."

"Something must be getting in the way."

"Perhaps it is." We continued searching for the missing piece that would pull the story together.

I tried to jettison the pain. Dr. Hammond and I again spoke to that two-year-old — a bit more firmly now, since two-year-olds, as we know, can be stubborn — and said, "You can go now. You can move on." We gave that two-year-old every advantage and the knowledge that our loving arms, mine and Dr. Hammond's, were there to guide her. And she wouldn't move. She couldn't move.

Instead, she fell flat on her face.

*　*　*

I continued talking to Dr. Hammond through November. Each day I would be just about able to glue myself together. I knew that I looked fine and acted fine, but even as I watched myself pretending to be fine I knew full well that I wasn't.

One day passing time before a phone session I took a walk through the woods to the General Store. As I headed down the hill to the store, I started to feel panicky and then in my mind's eye saw my two- or three-year-old self, as I recalled from a photograph, sitting and bawling while a lump lay next to her. *The baby.* I recalled hearing some story of how, as a young child, I had let the latch off my baby brother's crib and he had fallen out. This seemed to be a screen memory of that event, incorporating the scene and the panic and the horrid guilt over what I had made happen.

I was in a state of abject terror when I put the call in to Dr. Hammond. "Could this memory be why I sometimes have those awful fears about hurting my own child?" I asked. "Is this what my unconscious has been getting at?"

"Perhaps," she said, her voice cool as ever. "Let's see what else comes up."

We talked more of early childhood: of a little girl crying, thinking she hurt her baby brother, horror-stricken that her envious feelings towards him really were destructive, even lethal. Was this a restoration of an actual event, a memory reconstructed from the shreds of its remains? Or was this a story concocted as a rationale for the constant dread I was feeling, a narrative that had begun to take on a life of its own?

At the end of our session I felt terrible. "I wish I didn't have to explore this stuff. I wish it would go away," I said, growing aware that regardless of what was going on in my head, I soon needed to pick up Brendan at preschool, find some way to amuse him, go to the store and make dinner.

Dr. Hammond said: "I'm glad you had that memory."

Oh? She was? So maybe this was the huge revelation that needed to break into consciousness. Dr. Hammond must know. Maybe now everything would be okay. I waited for some internal shift toward the light.

It never came.

I knew things were bad. It had also begun to dawn on me that I needed to cut ties with Dr. Hammond. It was hard to convince myself she was there when I knew she was several states and an entire time zone away. We were trying to fool my psyche into believing she could remain an important figure in my life and it wasn't working. We couldn't keep this up. This treatment wasn't helping me. Indeed, it was destroying me. Yes — I could see that. The "journey" she was taking me on was a journey straight downhill. But where to turn? When pain or panic seized me, it was her number that I automatically dialed. Who else would understand what was going on with me? Who else could help me get better?

By now I was dealing with a full-fledged diagnostic entity: a clinical depression with anxious features. I was consistently hitting just about all the symptoms of Major Depressive Episode as noted in the DSM IV. I felt a constant darkness. I felt deep love for my family and yet walled off from them, as though I were sending them my love across a huge divide.

Every day I faced the clock with all of its hours strung out in one long, interminable line to be traversed. And yet I knew that there were too many things right in my life for everything to be so wrong.

I was reminded of those good things when I cuddled my son, a fluffy blond lapdog of a child. When I woke up to the sight of deer eating apples from a tree after a fresh snow, the apples bright and picturesquely red. When we enjoyed a good meal with my parents, big fans of Tony's cooking, which we could now do at an hour's notice. For domestic life went on as usual. I did my best to insulate Brendan and Tony from my moods. With Brendan, it was easy. My behavior with him seemed to arise out of some protected, healthy place, some reservoir of stability. As for Tony, I think he had simply gotten used to my distant, preoccupied bearing. And any frustration he felt was tempered by concern.

One night in early December I knew, the instant the light went out, that I would be awake until morning. I lay in bed and looked at my husband and my son, who at some point joined us, and from within the great void of my being thought about how much I loved them. As I lay, numb and wretched, I listened to the soft, rhythmic chant of their breathing and watched the slow choreography of their dreams. I envied the innocence of their slumber. I wished I could crawl into it with them, the way I had crawled under the down comforter against the chilly night. Then I thought: I can't continue this way. These two men, big and little, were the true center of my life. I needed to find my way back to them. It was either my family or Dr. Hammond. I had to give up one or the other.

The next day I called Dr. Hammond and left a message saying that I wanted to cancel our scheduled telephone appointment and discontinue therapy. I felt giddy with the boldness of the move I had just made. My defiance gave me a boost, a temporary one I knew but hoped it would at least carry me through my decision. I busied myself around the house thinking, alternately, "I don't want to talk to her!" and "Did she forget me or something? When is she going to call!?" She got back to me later that day and, with proper concern and cordiality, invited me to explain why I had so abruptly decided to stop our treatment.

That was a good question. It sounded so silly when she said it. Then an uncomfortable, weighty feeling in my stomach reminded me of why. I held my ground. "I really don't want to get into it," I said.

I really didn't. I was afraid I'd be lured into the familiarity of our conversations, that I'd be tempted to join her in analyzing this rash decision of mine. Boy, that could give us fodder for weeks of treatment! Resistance, rebellion, rage, what else? And then there was my story. How could I just up and leave in the middle just as things might really be getting good and juicy? I didn't want any more enticement. Hadn't I been here before and never reached the promised denouement?

There was a strange sensation of emptiness on the line between us, an emptiness I would normally fill with some disquisition of my fears, some confession of my real feelings, some deferment to her better judgment. She held the line an instant longer, no doubt taken aback by my unaccustomed silence, and said good-bye to me.

The liberation I felt from acting on my convictions lasted about two minutes. I had hardly hung up the phone when my buoyant well-being fell with a thud. The utter desolation of my life struck me full force. I couldn't simply wash my hands of psychotherapy and move on, as I was undeniably depressed. I was stuck with the pain, but had now given up my crutch. And with that crutch, support. I clearly needed help, but didn't know what kind. Without my therapist, how could I give meaning to the pain? And without assigning meaning to the pain, how could I release it? Therapy had created the structure for my life. What would I be without it? I was winging it, made scarier by the fact that I had no wings.

While on a walk the next day I ran into Trudy, the head of psychological services on campus, a clinician who only weeks before I had talked to as a potential professional contact. She saw the expression on my face and quickly guided me into her office where I promptly plopped down on the couch and began to vent my torment while trying to impress on her that I knew what was happening. "I can't get out of all these old two-year-old feelings," I said. "It's as though I'm permanently regressed."

Trudy looked at me with alarm. "Nobody should be doing that kind of work over the telephone," she said firmly. Even though I knew Dr. Hammond had used poor judgment, I felt oddly defensive of her and was tempted to make excuses on her behalf. Trudy kept to business: she recommended that I call an MD to get started on a proper trial of medication, and, for support, a local therapist.

I called the therapist, Sherri, and set up an appointment because I knew I needed a human being beyond my poor overwhelmed family members to be there for me. However it was painful going to meet her, driving half an hour through the mountains to get there, knowing that I could not allow myself even the illusion that she could cure me. I had begun to see that taking a pick-shovel to my unconscious was not the way for me to get healthy.

But it was so tempting. Sherri was a good listener. A petite woman with short brown hair and glasses, she had a friendly, impish smile. The office was pleasant and homey. The couch so soft and inviting. If I could just give Sherri my story, if I could ask her to fill in the gaps once and for all, if I could share some of the burden of my feelings with someone else. She was so nice. And that caring, permissive expression. How well I knew it. I have worn it myself.

I resisted. "I will never again give another person that much power over me," I told Sherri, holding fast to the last shreds of my strength.

"You shouldn't," she said.

The fact was, therapy was more than a crutch: it had become my entire way of life, my religion. In severing my tie with Dr. Hammond, it was as though I had cut off my source of air, which fueled and sustained me. In regarding Sherri as just another person and not a savior — which took will — I was not just turning down the chance to be helped but turning my back on how I had framed and defined my world: as a psychotherapy patient. I free-associate, therefore I am. What else was there? And could I last long enough to find out? It was both psychological and *ontological* free fall.

Therapy had given me a sense of purpose. One readily sanctioned by our culture. For wasn't self-improvement a valuable thing to devote energy to? Wasn't "know thyself" a respected aim? And in giving up the belief that exploratory, analytical psychotherapy was the means to contentment, I also needed to relinquish the role of the literary in mental health. Oh, I didn't want to give that up. I wanted to believe that feeling and narrative went together. I wanted to believe that if I doggedly worked through my story, interpreting and reinterpreting key events, not only would I heal but it would all make sense. I wanted to believe that the apt phrase, the precise rendering of subjective feeling states, held the power to transform. I was infatuated with psychotherapy as a form, as a *genre.*

Most of all I wanted to feel better. But I didn't know what better was. Nor how to get there.

*   *   *

I met with Sam Randall, MD, at his office near the hospital. He didn't know quite what to make of my situation in the time we had, but he was clear that depression had a good deal to do with it. He scratched his beard, in that quintessential pose of control and confusion, and prescribed for me Ativan for anxiety to take as needed and one of the new-and-improved dual-action antidepressants.

I then headed off to San Diego for our annual visit with Tony's mother, with the hope that it would work. I counted off the days until the medication should start to take effect but nothing happened, not even any side effects. Whatever that drug contained seemed to slip, unnoticed, past the appropriate neurological connections. Surrounded by family and yet alone, I walked along the beach and scanned the pleasant boutiques, a dark speck amidst the sunshine.

One infuriating thing about Southern California is that you're bombarded with the notion that everything you could ever want is within your grasp. Well-dressed, well-aerobicized people amble by, looking for things to spend their plentiful money on. The light renders cars so bright and shiny it's easy to think that buying the latest model could make you happy. Everyone is actively improving him- or herself.

One day I wandered into a bookstore that specializes in upbeat California New Age. There I was, surrounded by possibility. Perhaps somewhere on these shelves was a formula, phrase, or suggestion that could give me relief. I found a child's-type picture book on how to get past emotional pain. One page, where the stick-figure person was huddled over beside a rough triangle of a mountaintop, read "Cry, and know that you're not alone." Who else read these books, I wondered? Did they have real losses to be pained over, or just this amorphous stuff like me? I thought of others feeling pain and imagined the world suffused with it, like San Diego's morning fog. Yes, other people hurt too. I left the store and tried to keep this wisdom with me. But far from making me feel better it left me feeling worse.

I chatted with my brother long distance. It was nighttime in London and late morning for me. Fred filled me in on what his family was up to and how his work was going. As usual, he was frustrated that he wasn't getting enough done but, also as usual, he seemed to be producing a good deal of scholarship in spite of this. With a new baby, Benjamin, in addition to Julius, he and Carin were outgrowing their apartment. They were looking at houses in Muswell Hill, a neighborhood on the frontier of affordable housing, just beyond the underground line.

He asked how I was.

"Well," I said. "I'm in a bit of a rough place, but I think I just need to work things through — stuff that has come up in therapy — and I'm in some pain about things from the past, some unconscious stuff, really. I really just need to work this out. Do you know what I mean?"

There was a pause. "No," he said, not without concern. "No, Judy, I really don't."

For a while the music we had running in the car on our idle junkets was a collection of the blues singer Taj Mahal. One song in particular, "Giant Step", spoke to me. Stop clinging to the past, the song says. Get out of your head. Take a big leap away from that "lonely room" with its misery and memories and rejoin the rest of the world.

When this song came up Tony and I would stop whatever conversation we were having and listen. There was something about Taj Mahal's gravelly voice that was earthy and true. When we were out of the car Tony would mouth those words to me: Get out of your head. Rejoin the world.

Oh, Tony, if I could.

By this point he and I had run out of ways to talk about what was happening. My wretchedness went beyond the empathy and understanding we usually shared. For the most part we talked around it, communicating the essentials to get through each day (errands to run, Brendan's needs). Taj Mahal at least had given Tony some words, a soundtrack to his alienation from me. He wanted me with him. He wanted me back.

Oh Tony, I would go with you, I would go with you anywhere, in a flash. But I couldn't leave that lonely room.

About two weeks into our trip, just after Christmas, my mother-in-law fell during the night. She cut her head and, even more seriously for someone approaching eighty, contracted pneumonia. Tony had noticed a light on in her room and found her sometime around 3:00 AM. An ambulance team, large men full of noise and official questions, came and took her to the hospital. Tony and my brother-in-law Ralph, a physician, followed.

This was terrifying for everyone. As was custom, Tony's entire family had converged on San Diego for the holidays and there were plenty of people there for help and mutual diversion. Liesel was in the hospital for several weeks — one week in intensive care. For a while the prognosis wasn't so good. They had trouble weaning her from the oxygen. We all just took it day by anxious day.

In some remote chamber of awareness I was sad and worried. I loved this woman who was strong and wise and shared so many wonderful qualities with her son. In her own special way she was a matriarch, a quiet but constant moral presence. But I was so off-kilter that my own misery was front and foremost while this worrisome event was somewhere in the background. I tried to be helpful and strong for Tony but I was totally hollow. I took phone messages, filled and emptied the dishwasher, straightened up the mail and newspapers. A friend in the apartment building named Joel, someone Liesel checked in with every day, also came down with pneumonia and had been taken by ambulance to another hospital. I knew, at least intellectually, how serious this was.

My parents, of course, kept in touch with us about Liesel's condition, and sent flowers and a card. "You know," I said, trying to shift gears but not knowing how to do so effectively. "I'm not doing so well, either."

"What's going on?" my mother asked, her voice dropping a register.

I tried to explain. I didn't want to worry them, but I thought they should know that I was in bad shape, beyond just feeling a little blue, beyond the usual griping they were used to. They assured me that they would always be there for me. Well yes, that meant a lot to me, but...

I had Tony talk to them. He took the phone into the other room and was gone for several minutes. "I don't think they understand," Tony said wearily after he got off the phone. "I'm not sure that they can." However, my parents continued to dutifully call every day, to check on both of us patients.

It was awful to be in the midst of a family crisis and feel nothing. I felt useless. More than useless, I felt a burden to all by my very presence. I felt so awful that I wanted to die. I decided to put a call in to Dr. Randall and sent Brendan off to the beach with my niece and nephews; I was sure he would be well-coddled and well-amused. While I was waiting for the call back I started making a chicken soup for Joel, who was now home but had no family nearby. I wanted to do something, do some good for someone.

The phone rang. Oops — let me turn the heat down on that soup. My hands smelling of chicken fat, I told Dr. Randall, "I want to *off myself.*" (I was feeling that. That's why I called, right?)

"Judith, you have a small child. A two-year-old."

"I still can't believe that," I whimpered.

"He needs you. You can't let your son grow up without a mother."

More whimpering.

"Do you have a suicide plan?"

"No."

"Do you know where to go locally if things get really bad?"

"Yes." (The hospital. I had looked into this.)

He said not to stint on the Ativan and that we'd look into other medications when I returned. I said thanks and good-bye. I went back to my soup. Nothing made any sense.

A few moments later the door burst open and the gang streamed in. "Hey, it smells great in here!" "We walked all the way to Flat Rock!" "Boy is Brendan heavy. I carried him half the way back!" Four fresh, glowing faces. My son: the brightest one of all.

Yes, I wanted to be helpful. I volunteered to go to the drugstore to pick up antibiotics for Liesel; filling prescriptions was something I certainly knew how to do. I drove to the closest of a series of shopping centers along Del Mar Heights Road. In the already dark late afternoon the road with its brightly-lit homes looked like an overgrown Christmas decoration, the six lanes going up and then down the hill like a loop in a ribbon. I waited in line, basking in my momentary usefulness. I saw a well-dressed, nicely made-up woman filling a prescription for Depakote. That would be for bipolar disorder. I wondered if that would help me? I wanted to go up to her and ask, "How do you like it?" as if comparing brands of detergent in a TV commercial.

The Ativan provided an escape hatch. It took the edge off the pain and blunted the panic. But still I wrestled over every half pill I took. Maybe I would just hold out for another hour or two.

"Listen to your doctor," Tony scolded when he saw me miserable. "You've got to take it when you need it. And take enough." But I kept thinking I could tough it out, and was afraid of becoming dependent on the pills. This was ironic when I consider how willingly I had allowed myself to become dependent on a therapist.

We extended our stay twice and then Tony wanted to remain longer to look after his mother once she came out of the hospital. She needed constant care. I didn't feel well enough to go back to Vermont and care for Brendan alone — I hardly knew anyone there at that point, aside from everything else — so I went back to Chicago and stayed with my friend Cathy, whose son, Colin, was born just two hours after Brendan at the same hospital and delivered by the same obstetrician.

This was a blurry, broody week. Brendan got an ear infection and I held him on my lap as he slept between doses of bubble-gum flavored syrup. I saw friends, all in motion, all doing regular-life things, while I remained paralyzed. I showed them pictures of our rented house in Vermont and they oohed and ahhed at its rustic charm while they made excuses for my unhappiness. "Moving that far must be so hard." "I'm sure living in a rural area takes a while to get used to." I kept saying I loved it, but why would they believe me? I slouched around on Cathy's sofa for long periods of time in awe of the simple competence she showed by cooking a meal or sweeping the floor. The hours dragged by while waves of pain surged over me and receded, surged and receded, throughout the day.

Cathy had been a nurse and knew how to take care of me without condescension. She offered company without pushing it, which I greatly appreciated. She knew I appreciated her, though I couldn't show much. In part we were sustained by the shared fantasy that our sons, at two-and-a-half not much interested in socializing, would create a friendship that mirrored ours.

Between chores and feedings and naptimes we talked about how while I couldn't blame my mental state entirely on psychotherapy, it certainly hadn't helped. "That's what drives me crazy about that kind of therapy," Cathy said. "It's all digging, no planting. Like a garden where you keep pulling things up but never put anything in to grow."

Tony called every night to keep me up to date on his mother. She was recovering, but slowly. He also tried to read how I was doing from my tone of voice. "You sound a bit better today. Are you?"

I wanted to say yes. I wanted to please him, give him good news. But I also didn't want to lie. I didn't know if I was better. The answer usually depended on how recently I had taken the Ativan.

I knew the huge responsibility Tony was dealing with now. He had arranged a visiting nurse during the day but was on call all night, checking in on his mother and taking her to the bathroom or getting her a drink. I knew that due to his love for his mother he could handle this with dignity. My uselessness to him pained me. I mentally paired him off with every one of my friends, convinced that my wonderful husband would be better off with any of them than with me.

And yet, at any given moment I could stop, muster all my emotional energy and say to myself: the situation cannot possibly be as awful as it feels right now. Something was wrong here, and it wasn't only me. I could hold onto such clarity for but a short time, however, for within minutes some other random worry would unnerve me and I would crash back down again.

Sometimes I would revert to the habit of thumbing through that handy old psychological history of mine. I was doing this over the phone with Nina when she interrupted me and offered this advice: "Don't try to figure anything out. Just get better. Remember: you need to feel okay before you can feel okay."

I decided to see Dr. Hammond. Despite cutting off contact I still felt a strong connection to her, even if partially in defiance. I was aware of when she was on vacation (predictable from year to year) and mentally kept tabs on her schedule (Dr. Hammond would be in the office this morning...) And I admit: there was a part of me that held onto the notion that she could perform some magic and make it all better; a spark of a fantasy that she alone held the key to my recovery. I told myself that this appointment was for "closure", knowing very well that wasn't all of it.

So like countless times before over the past two years, I made the short drive to her office, this time in Cathy's dark green mini-van riding high above the snowy road. I was bundled up in Cathy's clothes and nearly tripping in borrowed snow boots. I had packed for Southern California. My winter stuff was back home.

I sat the standard two minutes in the waiting room and then Dr. Hammond opened the door. Yes, she was still there; life had gone on without me. I had this sense that one could come into this office any time, day or night, rain or snow or ten years from now, and she would still be sitting here, pulling her skirt over her knees (the closest thing to a nervous tick one could accuse her of), eternally affirming and accepting. She looked the same, her professional demeanor intact. I, on the other hand, was in worse shape than ever.

"How are things for you?" she asked with studied nonchalance.

"I've been seriously depressed," I said, stating the obvious but making a statement nonetheless.

She looked at me, all sternness and seriousness, and said, "You are not depressed. You are *angry* with me."

*　*　*

Back in Vermont, Dr. Randall expressed concern that mine might not such be a straightforward case. So he tactfully extricated himself from the situation and referred me to someone else. (I'd never been rejected by a shrink before. Was it something I said?) So one Friday afternoon in late January I made my way northward through a snowstorm to see Stephen Cole, MD, a psychiatrist associated with Sherri's group practice.

After a long wait, during which I had the chance to read everything I could ever want to about making maple syrup, Dr. Cole, a tall, slender, somewhat bookish-looking man, came to fetch me. I followed him up the cramped stairs to his office and settled myself down while he opened his briefcase and released a spray of papers. He bent over to pick them up from the floor and knocked a stack of notepads off the desk. Oh great, I thought. A nerd.

While my new psychiatrist was collecting himself, I thought about how I wanted to present. Do I start with the messed up stuff? Or do I first show that I'm reasonable and savvy about psychotherapy? I was about to get into that seeing-a-shrink rhythm, that codified show-and-tell. After a moment, Dr. Cole leaned toward me, looked at me intently, and said, "Why are you here?" Befitting my emotional state, I tried to say everything at once.

"You've got a problem," he said. "But I've seen worse."

He was not interested in psychodynamic details. Instead, with our remaining time he gave me fill-in-the-blank tests for depression, obsessive-compulsive-disorder (OCD), and Attention Deficit Disorder (ADD). "You said you have trouble concentrating," he said. "We may as well rule it out." This was deflating. There was no room for any of my insight and subtlety. But I went with it. And I got a jolt of familiarity with some of the questions for OCD: "Do you frequently seek reassurance? Doubt what you say or do? Have intrusive thoughts?" (Please, I don't want to go there...)

"You talk about feeling regressed," he said. "That's a *psychodynamic* term. I'm thinking biologically here and I would say you're *depressed.* Let's stick to the medication and see what happens."

He said that since the Paxil, at a fairly low dose, was never fully given a chance, it might make sense to try another SSRI. He prescribed Luvox, which he had had good success with for depression and obsessive compulsive disorder, and Ativan to take as needed to get through the nights.

All that weekend I went over the encounter in my mind. Though I'd stopped believing that psychodynamic interpretations held the cure, I couldn't quite stop myself from making them. I was like a machine that kept running a while after being turned off. I tried to "process" our meeting, processing being what enlightened, therapist-types did after any meaningful exchange; the failure to process meant being ignorant and oblivious. Did I sense some transference here? Did I want to impress Dr. Cole by being a good patient and buying into the medical framework? Did I want just to let him take care of me? I was boring myself with the tedium of these thoughts even as they rambled on, seemingly of their own accord.

So, armed with yet another new batch of pills, I embarked on another waiting period, a long phase of holding my breath. I started reading a bit about psychopharmacology. I browsed in bookstores and the library, going over words like serotonin and neurotransmitters as though memorizing the rules of a club I was to join. I was looking for something to hold onto and would take it wherever I could. I was increasingly baffled as to why Dr. Loftus had never fully informed me about psychotropic medications and the trial-and-error often necessary to find the right one in the right dose. I recalled bitterly what he had said to me: *"Don't use this medication to avoid your real problems"*.

I met once a week with Sherri, but it felt like we were merely marking time. I would drive north on Vermont Route 7, the road often to myself in mid-day hours, noting by the play of light on the snow how close I was to Manchester. Just before the turn-off was a spot where light fell in cascading lines, like wool on a loom. Once there I'd sit on Sherri's plush couch and say, somewhat aimlessly, "So you think this stuff is going to work, huh?" I wasn't going to get pulled into any psychodrama. She wasn't my mother, my guru, my savior.

"Yes," she'd answer. "If not this particular drug, then another one. I've seen it happen again and again."

"Well, what's going to happen?"

"One day you'll feel not quite so awful. And then another day you'll feel less awful. And then one day you won't feel awful at all. In fact, you might even feel pretty good."

"That sounds delightful," I'd sigh, glancing about at the Vermont crafts and antiques strewn tastefully about the room: what a lovely setting for serenity.

I realized the medium I was dealing with right now was not *story*; it was *time* — however long it took to find a medication that works. I accepted how little control I had over this. In previous therapy I had overestimated the degree of volition I had. Knowing that I was at the mercy of the pain I felt offered one kind of relief but was frightening in a different way.

In early February I saw a notice in the local paper about an interfaith healing service. People who were ill and suffering as well as those taking care of them were invited to attend. It was held at the local synagogue, home to a small, active congregation where I had been a few times and where I already knew I would be comfortable. I decided to go.

It turned out to be a beautiful service. There was a sizeable group, by Vermont standards at least, mostly elderly women and men. The rabbi and a minister spoke about the healing traditions of Judaism and Christianity and we sang a few simple prayers. At the end each person walked up to light a candle and present a silent prayer. The mood was intimate but respectful.

One song began with a chant, *"Ana El na, rafa na lah,"* Moses' prayer to heal his sister Miriam. We sang:

Please God, heal her.
Please God, heal him.
Please God, heal us.
Please God, heal me.

Then back to the refrain, sung in that kind of stirring ancient melody that transports you through time.

The incidental harmony of so many amateur and faltering voices singing in unison moved me to tears. I wasn't so alone, it seemed. People suffered in so many different ways. I didn't have to wrestle my own story in isolation. I could be part of a communal one.

The rabbi nodded at me; in a small town every new face is noted. I had mentioned to him that my mother-in-law had been ill. I'm sure he assumed that's why I was there. Although I am now an active member of the synagogue, I have never told him the truth: I wasn't there for my mother-in-law. I wasn't there as a counseling psychologist broadening my clinical repertoire. I was there for myself.

*　*　*

One morning I was on my way to my appointment with Sherri when I felt my wheels slide. Snow had drifted onto the highway entrance and the road was slippery. As far as I could see wind was sweeping snow onto the road. This was not a day to be driving. Appointment or not, I wanted to get home. I couldn't remember ever skipping a therapy appointment. Usually I was so desperate I would have forged my way through an avalanche. But I don't really need this session, I thought as I turned around, pleased enough to have a good excuse to take time to myself and very happy to be safe.

"I think I'm feeling a little less miserable," I tentatively told Sherri at our next appointment.

"Yes, I see a difference in you today," she said, trying to contain her optimism. "A brightness."

"Do you think it's — "

"We don't know. Let's just see."

"Maybe I don't need to come in next week."

"Okay. But call if you need to."

I stopped needing the Ativan to get to sleep, even when I woke up in the middle of the night. And over the weekend an amazing thing happened. On Sunday I woke up with a vaguely pleasant feeling. I mused over the day ahead — cross-country skiing might be nice; hmmm...I wonder if we had ingredients for pancakes. Did we use up that buttermilk? — before I even realized the momentous thing that was happening to me. I wasn't hurting. I wasn't fretting. Something was relaxing inside me.

I let myself feel that. I could sense an entire constellation of internal experience dissolving. In that very instant — when it became clear to me that the medication was having an effect — the story of my life, the story I had crafted over so many 50-minute hours, began to reconfigure itself.

It is hard to convey what a strange experience this was. It was as if there was a train pulling out of the station and the visitors were still there, loitering about, but they weren't quite fully there either. This was a moment of dynamic transfer: the train (my life) would be moving off to a new place. The old station (my former biochemical environment and all that went with it) would retreat into the past. Its surroundings, its air, its mood would slip into memory.

All that day I could feel the movement into new terrain. I could glance back and see the grayness of the old, dreary scenery. I could see that the source of that gray, my symptoms, in all their lifelong variations, all stemmed from a similar source, an errant bad feeling ever looking for a place to roost. Like constantly forming and reforming clouds, this mass of sensation would assume different shapes and aspects but never, or only momentarily, fully disperse.

I also understood how the bulk of my energy had gone into managing my emotional state, trying to maintain some psychic equilibrium. I had a constant vigilance over what I felt, a tendency to monitor myself that Dr. Hammond said I was ready to give up. I couldn't have given it up. It was wired into my being. I knew that now.

Yes I had had a problem. But that problem wasn't "psychological". I now began to question yet further the project Dr. Hammond and I were collaborating on. Those painful fears — of suicide, of hurting my child, of being "bad" — weren't material for therapy. The painful, almost nauseating anguish wasn't necessarily "a feeling I had survived before." These were *symptoms*. On medication my mind didn't pull those old tricks. That darkness was one aspect of an illness. The anguish, another. These were biochemical accidents. Non sequiturs.

Likewise the story we devised was not the sum total of personal truth, but a narrative created to try to explain this illness, not unlike the way primitive cultures created fables to explain thunder and lightning. Of course this notion would have been heresy to me but a few months before.

In her famous essay on internal/external chaos, "The White Album", Joan Didion opens with the line, "We tell ourselves stories in order to live." For indeed, if we feel we can make sense of our lives, we can live with ourselves. With my own clients I would say, as an intervention, "there is a way to make sense of this." This was in lieu of saying, "everything will be all right," which, much as I wanted to, I knew I could not say.

Live with myself. That's what my story, co-written by Dr. Hammond, Linda, and others allowed me to do. No more and no less. It maintained the status quo, rather than change it. When ill, one clings to the story for survival. That's what happened to me. And I was so immersed in it that I missed the real truth: that I had a mood disorder.

The details I came up with weren't necessarily inaccurate, in that they did derive from experience and perceptions. But I now understand that they were, almost by definition, skewed. If we could call mood a kind of music, I only picked up the low tones and set everything in a minor key.

Psychologists have a term for this: "mood-congruent memory retrieval." When you're happy you tend to remember happy things; when you're sad you remember sad things. A related concept is "state-dependent memory retrieval." When you're emotionally aroused (anxious, angry, etc.) you're likely to recall experiences that occurred when you were in a like state. Because I was in constant turmoil I remembered all the times I had been in turmoil and those memories drowned out the rest. In part this was because, scientists have found, in recalling an emotional memory one re-experiences those feelings physiologically, down to the neurotransmitters and the release of stress hormones like catecholamines and cortisol.

Did my early childhood experiences and relationships cause longstanding discomfort? Probably to some extent. Clinically, however, it's irrelevant: beyond a certain point, trying to revise that narrative was futile. Given what I know about family history, the depression and anxiety were likely genetic. Why didn't I or any clinician give serious attention to that possibility? Why did everything have to be metaphor?

After the train started moving, with a few minor jerks and jolts as it gained traction, I could look back on the landscape and see the lifelong mixed depression and anxiety for what it was. I could observe it from a distance, clinically even. One way to describe it is that I had felt as if caught between two mirrors facing each other, locked in eternal gaze. Or trapped in a glass bubble, unable to get out. Dissecting my own story was not a cure for my illness, but a symptom of it. I was never able to attend outward; I couldn't lose myself in the flow of experience. Inward was the only way my mind went. I could now begin to forgive myself for not fixing myself that way.

I can't emphasize this enough: it's hard to know what being okay is if you've never experienced it. As my friend Nina put it, you need to feel okay in order to feel okay.

I now discovered a middle ground of mood, neither too up nor too down. I felt that I had found within me that essential but elusive Self.

Yes, there was a sturdy entity that was me; it wasn't so wobbly anymore. I no longer felt the portent of my grandmother's suicide, her sad fate tugging at me like an undertow. I could feel love for my family for what it was. I learned to move around in this new emotional state, the way you get used to a new house, figuring out where you like to sit, which spots get the best light. I had the capacity to attend outside of myself. Rather than restlessly waiting for time to pass I could let go of self-consciousness, as if dropping anchor.

☆ ☆ ☆

Alas, I had more trials ahead. The dose I was taking proved not to be high enough and I lost the response. I swear there was a moment when I felt the wires snap. I grieved the new Self I had discovered as I had grieved so many things and set to work with Dr. Cole to adjust the medication. I felt so let down, so *betrayed*, I said to him, struggling against despair. He looked directly at me and without flinching said: "My patients get better."

I allowed myself to be reassured.

The higher dose was too high — it gave me an awful, agitated buzz — so we tried a dose in between. Nothing. Then we kept the lower level and added BuSpar, an anti-anxiety medication that builds up in the system like an antidepressant. This was to function as a booster, a medication that intensifies the effect of an antidepressant when someone can't tolerate a higher dose. It boosted me too much and I felt high. I giggled through the Passover Seder. (*Why is this night different?*) A little more of this, a little less of that. There was a week when I woke up in a different mental state every day: racy, weepy, sleepy, dopey. I had no clue about what to expect. "Ride it out," said Sherri and Dr. Cole. "Just ride it out."

Ultimately it clicked. Then a spell of reckoning: how to fully grasp that for the first time in my life I was on an even playing field with the rest of humanity? What did it mean to accept that I had an illness? What was it all about?

Yes, what *is* my life all about, I pondered as I did chores, folded laundry, walked Brendan to and from preschool. I asked this question as I rode my bicycle along the country roads on a beautiful day in June, my birthday, anticipating a potluck dinner being held in my honor. That night several of us had dinner by candlelight on the synagogue school-building porch. I was touched but a bit tentative; I still felt new in town. At one point the rabbi's wife was talking about how it had taken her a while to feel comfortable with Reconstructionist Jewish practice. She wasn't born to the faith; her father was a Baptist minister. "At first I worried about what I should believe," she said. "But then I saw that what was important was the *doing*. You do the rituals and prayer, be open to the experience, and through the doing it will begin to make sense."

Oh — that's how it worked. I didn't have to ascribe meaning to my life. Life acquires meaning through the doing.

Mostly, what I make of things is that I am incredibly fortunate to live in a time when biochemical imbalances can be treated. This awareness keeps me humble. Rather than imagining my grandmother as a madwoman in the attic to be hidden away I envision a lovely, intelligent woman — she raised my father and my uncle (two good men, two doctors) in spite of her suffering — who, as a reflection of genetics, may have faced struggles not unlike my own. It saddens me that I know so little about her, as though the mark of incurable depression simply erased her existence. I want to be able to revive her memory, celebrate what she has given our family even as we mourn what could have been. I want to call back across time and let her know that I don't take her suffering, or my good fortune, for granted.

I also regret the blame I put on my parents through my years of treatment. My therapists' assessment of family dynamics were probably pretty well on-target — the defenses and deflections, our alliances and misalliances — but even so they could not explain the pain. Sure my parents are imperfect, in some ways endearingly, in some ways less so. But I could also see that the family is indeed nice in ways that are not merely repressed anger, aggression, or envy, but that reflect good will and love.

Here's a new twist: when I searched for explanations for my unhappiness through therapy I assumed that my upbringing was *the* problem. (And there was always just enough truth, bells of recognition hit just often enough.) I now see I was ill — and it was aspects of that very upbringing that allowed me to be as functional as I was. And oh, how difficult it must have been to be the parent of a child that couldn't, wouldn't, be consoled.

I don't mean to say that people should resolve all their problems with pills. I know that attitude now dominates, and that the complexity of people's needs is getting short shrift. Human connection is essential, and some people need help in finding ways to connect. But beyond a point it's cruel to tell someone he can break through emotional pain or else it's a moral failure.

Not only that, but slogging through painful affect can actually make things worse. Research in neurobiology has shown how repeated emotional responses literally become etched in the brain. It's a lot like walking in the snow. The more times you walk a trail — and for some reason you're always drawn to follow your own footprints, despite all that white space — the more packed down the path.

By repeatedly exercising the neural connections associated with troubling memories ("Let's go back into that early pain...") I was in a real, physiological sense strengthening that response. Dr. Hammond and I were digging a rut in my brain's memory tracks. In time I got dug in so deep that I couldn't see out.

It is amazing what science can tell us about what goes on in our minds. No doubt this knowledge will offer new, more effective ways to ease psychological pain. No doubt medications like SSRIs represent just the beginning. There's also EMDR (Eye Movement Desensitization and Reprocessing) in which a person recalls a painful memory while receiving some kind of rhythmic sensory stimulation (typically alternating sounds or the therapist moving her hand back and forth.) The theory is that traumatic events aren't properly processed and stored (which helps explain why such memories feel so raw) and the bilateral stimulation aids in information processing. Plus, research suggests that traumatic events impair the brain hemispheres' capacity to work in concert. By engaging both the right and left brain, this treatment helps weave together both brain hemispheres. Increasingly, clinicians are talking about brain-based treatments that draw on our young but growing understanding of neurobiology.

While this sounds like a huge departure from tradition it is worth remembering that Freud, Jung, and company were primarily scientists. They did what they could with observation, hypnosis, and crude instruments like the galvanometer (a device that measures physiological responses to stimuli, an early version of the lie detector test.) They might not have so patiently sat by the couch had they enjoyed the benefit of research tools like Magnetic Resonance Imaging (MRIs), Positive Emission Tomography (PET), and Quantitative Electro-encephalography (QEEG).

I will say this much: when I read about brain science, as I increasingly am inclined to do, I often get the same kind of "aha!" as I did when coming to a powerful realization in therapy.

I am extremely glad that I found this medication when I did and had the depression and anxiety under control by the time Brendan turned three. He was two-and-a-half when we made that last trip to Chicago. He still remembers the time that I "went to see that lady" and he watched television with our hosts. Though I spoke little of it, he picked up that this meeting was important to me.

Another time, when I was experimenting to find the right dose, I felt so awful that when my across-the-orchard friend and her little girl stopped by to join us on the porch I couldn't help but dissolve into tears. Brendan continues to ask, "Why did you cry with Hilary that day?"

He's a sensitive, inquisitive child and I'm happy that I don't need to burden his sensitivity with my own. I can be fully present for him in a way that I wouldn't have been, try as I may, without medication.

* * *

Vermont's spring was exquisite and sudden. We had to wait a good while for it, this is true, but when spring came it arrived with broad strokes of color and life. From one day to the next I would watch the trees by our house fan out into leaf; what from my office window seemed but a few measly twigs turned into a graceful, slender tree. With each drive to Brendan's preschool I'd see the mountains magically transformed in their colors and in their contours. At first all was a fresh, delicate green. Then the shade deepened to a darker, richer green. Change swept through our landscape with speed. I felt that the season and I had just been introduced.

We held Brendan's third birthday party on an uncommonly warm Sunday in May in the large walled garden on campus known as the "Secret Garden", visible from our house. We invited his class of nine preschoolers and their parents. My parents served as co-hosts. We cleaned the house furiously but the weather was so fine that no one got the benefit of our mop-and-broom work. Our one ambitious planned activity was a scavenger hunt, and all the children searched our special hiding places — next to the group of daffodils, under the bench beside the plum tree — to find their prizes, plastic zoo animals. Each child found a lap to sit on as Brendan tore the paper off his gifts and then we all shared the inevitably lopsided homemade chocolate cake topped with melting ice cream.

We joined the cooperative farm. With great anticipation, some forty families collected the first yield of the season: a handful of snap peas; some radishes and a fist-sized ball of lettuce. We held onto our grand ambitions. We cheered the garden on.

As summer approached people around town began to share their tips about the best swimming ponds. We debated whether it made sense to buy a season's pass to the local lake or pay for tickets one at a time. Tony and I discussed the wisdom of buying a canoe.

Someone I had lost touch with for eight years tracked me down and I got a contract to co-author a book.

* * *

What about my promising new career? Oh that's right: I was going to be a therapist. I cannot now imagine myself setting up shop and donning that mantle of knowing neutrality. I try but can't picture myself in stylish-but-not-showy clothes befitting my therapist persona, engaged in a teté-a-teté with a near-stranger's private soul. After what I experienced I'm chastened. I wonder: who am I to intrude on someone's story, to take a red pen to another person's inner life?

I know that therapy can cross the line between being helpful and being hurtful. How would I trust myself to determine that threshold? Clinicians often miss seeing it, I learned. Instead of saying "You've had enough therapy. Let's get another perspective," each therapist said, "Obviously your *last therapist* wasn't good enough." It's just like when you get a haircut and the stylist says, "Who last did your hair? It's all wrong!" I understand the temptation. As a clinician, there's no cheaper and easier shortcut to bonding with a client than to ally against a previous clinician. "*She* obviously didn't understand you." Implication: "*I* will."

I think about my clients. I think about Lucy and her Filofax, Marta and her men, Ellen and her crusades. I think about my clients at the Center as they grappled with the pressures and temptations of college life. I am grateful for the trust they placed in me. I am grateful for all that they taught me. I do believe I was helpful to them. I certainly *want* to believe I was.

If we assume that I did do some good, I couldn't say whether it came from the suggestions, interventions, and inferences I made or simply the fact that I sat in a room with a client, listened, and cared. Should I have known more about medication, and about the myriad manifestations of depression and anxiety, things I only learned later through my own hard experience? Probably. And which proved most beneficial to the work I did: my clinical training or some orientation or sensitivity I already possessed? I don't know.

I wish I could just say that I was against psychotherapy altogether. It would make it all simpler. But ah, that would be *splitting* (that primitive emotional defense whereby everything is either all bad or all good) and I won't let myself get away with that. Therapy helps many people tremendously. Insights generated in therapy can help people look at their lives in a new way. It can be invaluable to have someone to listen to you, or the space to talk out personal questions. I don't believe we are designed to handle every challenge completely alone. Ideally, therapy is a form of teaching, giving someone the tools with which to face situations they find difficult.

And I know that there can be magic in the room. There is some kind of alchemy between two people when one offers care and the other trust. There is something that flickers between them and which can spark the process of change. I would never deny that there is power in psychodynamic psychotherapy. I wasn't *that* big a fool.

In retrospect I'm stunned by the arrogance in believing that through reason, determination, and an outlay of cash I could vanquish a lifelong depression, that if I kept flinging myself at the pain I could finally break through it. It's a caricature of American can-do spirit: with enough therapy and effort you can trump biology. I'm also uncomfortably aware of an underlying elitism: all you need is endless time and money and you can buy health. I recall a friend once quipped that in certain pricey neighborhoods in Manhattan's Upper East Side you need to show your psychotherapy patient card to even cross the street.

Perhaps if I lived elsewhere and had fewer family demands I would wrestle with this ambivalence and continue my training, becoming a better clinician as a result. But too much time has gone by and too much money spent. I've already asked too much of my family. And frankly, I'm weary of focusing on pain. I've dedicated enough time to digging at it with shovels and my bare nails. It's a delight *not* to think about pain.

Nor am I inclined to take on such responsibility. You just don't know what someone can handle. After all, experienced therapists made misjudgments about me. Clinicians often use the presence of an "observing ego", a capacity to separate yourself from what you're experiencing, as an indication of mental health and the ability to tolerate the rigors of deep personal analysis. In my case the observing ego couldn't stop observing — and thus was a sign of something wrong.

When you're a therapist and the light is flashing on your answering machine, you don't know if it's a request to reschedule an appointment or a suicide call. In the past I was already so internally burdened that such weight was congruent with my own mental state. Now it would be a jolt. Why do that to myself? Even now when I visit a friend who's a therapist and I know she needs to call a client, I get antsy. "Hey, don't you think you should try that line again?" I say, anxious, checking the clock, knowing how awful that person may feel waiting for the call while we finish our conversation. I have been on the other side.

Sometimes I'll resurrect my therapist persona, that knowing self I conjured up during training. There is pleasure in being calm and insightful, in detaching enough to note the psychological currents shifting beneath people's actions. Once a friend worried about a family event that threatened to be tense. I said, "It sounds as if this is someone who feels out of control himself and therefore tries to control things around him." She looked at me, suddenly silent — she hadn't actually given me enough information to know this. "You're right! Gosh, you're good," she said. I relished the praise, and allowed myself a moment of private smugness. In such moments I'd think, in the indulged wistfulness of allowing an opportunity slip by, "Hmm. Maybe I did miss my calling..."

I did learn useful things in therapy through the years, helping me to gain and apply self-confidence. I found ways to compensate for the underlying depression and anxiety. I got a clearer perspective on my family, which has helped me be more accepting and loving. It has given me a way of looking at relationships, and gotten me in the habit of pulling back and asking, "What's going on here?" when interactions get dicey. In therapy you get into the habit of looking at things more thoughtfully, and looking beneath superficial conversation for the meaning of others' words. Analyzing your own and others' behavior can help you develop empathy.

Were all those clinical hours a waste of time, something much worse, or something else altogether? What about those deeply personal insights that seemed to hit a bulls-eye? "Everything happens for a reason," some would say. "There must be a reason you went through all you did." But I won't allow myself the comfort of narrative threads so neatly tied. A lot happened, certainly, but not necessarily for a reason.

Looking back, I think all those insights and revelations kept me hooked on the process. After a while they stopped being meaningful. In truth, I kept having the same revelations over and over again albeit pitched and packaged slightly different each time. Ultimately the revelations became just part of a game. They led nowhere but back to the therapist's office.

Once on the medication those revelations became moot. I don't continually refer to my psychological history, as before. My moods make enough sense to me now. I'm happy when there's reason to be happy, sad when there's reason to be sad, and full of moral outrage when events around me warrant it. I'm not from moment to moment doing the mental equivalent of walking on coals. Did the pain that I went through have any inherent value? If I had received medical treatment years earlier, would anything have been lost?

Therapy deceived me into thinking that I was more in control of what was happening to me than in fact I was. It therefore served to stave off despair when I would have been most prone to feel it. Was that a benefit or a hindrance, given that I delayed pursuing medical help? Psychoanalytic theory is a good century old now. What do we really know about it? To what extent does the endurance of the institution of psychotherapy reveal about the healing power of human connection? To what extent does it reveal the human capacity to fool oneself?

And what about all those insights and epiphanies generated through the decades? Think of all those patients and analysands rising from velvet-covered chaises in Vienna and London and New York, from leather armchairs in suburban offices and hospital suites, from metal chairs in thin-walled cubicles in strip-malls. All those folks reaching over for the strategically-placed box of tissues, wiping away long-suppressed tears. All those bottoms squirming in their seats and those eruptions of nervous laughter upon confronting uncomfortable truths. All those men and women walking out of therapists' offices feeling not quite the same as they did before.

What about all those retrospective literary masterpieces — epic, tragic, antic — carefully assembled session by session? What about all that *chat*? Has it vanished into the breath that gave it voice? Has it brought change to the tellers of the tales, or just the illusion of flux? Is the dominant form of treating mental pain over the last hundred years ultimately a medical or a *literary* phenomenon?

More practically, at what point does the chatter cease being useful and start being dangerous? When does the talk start moving around and around in circles, spiraling upward into lofty irrelevance or downward into ever deepening despair?

Despite the disaster of my treatment, I'm sure my therapist meant well. She held to the clinical model, operating according to therapeutic truism that everything is grist for the mill. Boy was I with her there. I kept that mill churning. I gave my all to it. What I learned the hard way was: not everything is meant to be processed. And with that knowledge an entire system of belief crumbled before me.

To what extent did she become overly invested in my story? After all she devoted many clinical hours, plus added phone time, to my case. I would never want to minimize that. But perhaps as a result she began to identify with the characters and wanted the heroine to come out ahead. So we went on, Dr. Hammond filling practice hours and cashing my checks, me biding my time until the pain ebbed, both of us pretending against all evidence that the treatment was working.

Therapy has that hall of mirrors quality. Calling a therapist's bluff can immediately be labeled "resistance". Sudden, quick improvement may be called a "flight into health" to escape painful realities. A serious backslide may be explained as "regression in the service of the treatment". When at my lowest I told Dr. Hammond that I was depressed, she said, no, *I was angry with her.* She insisted upon seeing me strictly within the frame of the therapeutic relationship. In doing so, she elided the fact that she had become part of the problem.

The story that emerges in therapy is a product of the collusion between client and therapist. You work together to create a version that confirms each person's beliefs. After all, patients in Freudian analysis tend to have Freudian dreams. It's hard to resist this. I liked the courage Dr. Hammond saw in me. I liked her ultimate prognosis, a full, emotionally rich life. I chose to believe all of it. Storytelling in psychotherapy is a way of making meaning, but it's often manufactured meaning.

I do need to be honest — I played my therapist. Just as had happened to me with my own clients, Dr. Hammond played into my hand. I needed tons of support and after decades of practice knew how to get it; I could locate a sympathetic ear the way an alcoholic sniffs out a drink. It wasn't always conscious but when a session flagged I might dredge up a memory, observation, or telling detail that I suspected might revive her attention. As a subtext to the therapy she was molding me to be the client she wanted and I was training her to be the clinician I wanted. But my mission to please her became part of the problem, as it kept me from seeking other perspectives.

Still, when you pass hours in another person's company and share experience, there is a bond that develops out of sheer duration and proximity. The therapeutic relationship is supposed to be an "as if" relationship: through transference, you (the client) interact as if the therapist is a character in your real life. At what point does a small grammatical shift occur and it moves from as if to "*is*"?

* * *

I now go to see Dr. Cole every other month to get a refill for my prescription. I look forward to these visits as they give me an excuse to shop in Manchester. (In Bennington we pretend to disdain Manchester's outlet stores but actually like to go there.) For when I need to refill my prescriptions it is usually just about time to replenish my supply of moisturizer (a deal at the Lancôme outlet). I can win points with Tony by getting a cooler's worth of sliced meat, olives, and fresh mozzarella from Al Ducci's Italian deli. And one can never have too many pairs of little boys' socks.

I sit briefly in the waiting area and then Dr. Cole comes down and I follow him up the creaky stairs. We are solemn and silent. An observer may think that we're about to engage in an intense session of psychotherapy. I sit while he locates my folder, which usually involves unpacking the better part of his closet. "How are you doing?" he asks. "Good," I say. We are both quiet. We both know that this small innocuous word "good" represents a vast life change for me. I tell him how thankful I am. What else is there to say? We talk in general about medication, including what the research says about the newest ones on the market, much as I would have talked about therapy in the past. This consumes all of 25 minutes, and I leave, take a deep breath and reflect on how grateful I am for my good health. Then I hit the stores.

Since the medication, I have a new, much-revised tale about my healing. Here goes:

A writer becomes a psychotherapist because, she now realizes, she wants a way out of her own depression. The in-depth psychotherapy that is supposed to cure plunges her into such despair that she gives in to the depression she has fought for so long. She is granted some pills, to be swallowed twice a day. Within a few weeks, she emerges from the fog. She dips back in (there's no good story without some setback) but comes out again and she is finally okay. Yes, she is no longer in exile, but part of the world. She is now able to live if not happily-ever-after then at least happily-enough-most-of-the-time.

I had envisioned plenty of variations of the story, but this one sounds like a fairy tale.

Wait — this isn't where I wanted to be. In the debate between biological treatments and psychotherapy I was always rooting for the other side. I'm not one for easy answers. Taking antidepressants to feel better seemed like such a cop-out, an erasure of so much I had believed in.

And still do. Even though slapped with the reality that psychotherapy is far from benign, I still champion the examined life over the unexamined version. I still see the value of pursuing unconscious fears and motivations and appreciate the healing power of relationship. I still maintain the importance of challenging oneself to grow. It seems you can take the girl out of psychotherapy, but you can't take psychotherapy out of the girl. My *brain* may be biochemical but my *mind* is still psychological.

It does feel like some cosmic joke has been played on me. I was such a good patient. I did all the right things. But I saw what happened when a commitment to psychotherapy is taken to its logical conclusion and the result was not pretty.

I could never again sing the praises of therapy like an innocent; the disillusionment runs too deep. I know that therapists lose their innocence many times over; they see too much. But most have faith in what they do. I think of Bonnie and the others who tried to impart that faith to me, and how that faith carries them through. That's something I could never recreate.

Instead, I stand at on the sidelines of the profession I had wanted to join. I can talk about clinical topics and share ideas, but I am not of them. I still have that desire to help others but will have to find other ways to do so. The loss of my ideals saddens me. It would be nice if therapy had done the trick and those ideals could be sustained. And I'm sheepish about my wasted training and the time and care others devoted to it. I had gotten myself all dressed up for the role, but, as it turned out, I didn't go through with the part after all.

*   *   *

These days I sleep deeply and dream vividly. The medication generates a circadian rhythm as constant and forceful as the tides. On a given night I may have several sleep/wake cycles. I'll dream discreet sketches, like chapters. Upon waking I feel that I'm clawing my way up from the depths, working to get a grasp on consciousness.

This sleep is non-negotiable. If I get less than a full night's worth I feel it. I guard those hours. Dr. Cole explains that many people on such medications have rich dreams. The chemicals in them cleanse the brain circuitry so that any residual anxiety gets worked out. For once I'm not already frazzled when I begin each day.

The dreams I have are not epic or portentous. They tend to turn on one small detail from the day prior, or the kind of joke or verbal play I might share with Brendan in the morning and which he would enjoy.

"What did you dream?" Brendan will often ask upon waking. He is in our bed. At some point in the middle of the night, unnoticed, he would have trotted down the hallway and joined us, the light he insists upon in his room still on. "I had a dream that we were in Cape Cod staying at a hotel and we had pancakes and rice for dinner!" he might say. "Wasn't that funny? I had another funny dream where I met my friend Garrett in the bathroom! He was sitting on the toilet wearing a bathing suit and a swimming pool floating ring!"

I'd then share with him whatever story I had been treated to in the night. "I dreamt that Grampy gave me a big truck. It had one of those names like Tundra or Igloo or something that makes you think of cold, open spaces. I looked at this huge, unwieldy thing and thought, how am I ever going to drive this?" My uncle had generously given us a stick-shift car and my father kept checking in to see if I had finally learned how to drive it.

"That's funny!" Brendan exclaims, a connoisseur of the absurd.

Also funny, the pills I take sometimes appear in my dreams: losing them, finding them, trading them like gold. Deep in my psyche I'm continually replaying the course of healing, like an archetypal creation myth.

And of course, knowing all about Cinderella tales I do fear midnight — the prospect that the medication could fail on me and I'll be back to my old rags. It happened that one time early on. But the biological treatment has given me a frame. I know the medications available are becoming more effective and precise all the time and that reassures me. I would never again think of scrutinizing hidden moments in my history for relief.

Meanwhile, thanks to some luck — the cheaper, inferior house we had contracted to buy suffered a fire two days before we were to close; after finding other fire hazards we were able to extricate ourselves from the deal — and perhaps a bit of financial recklessness, we did purchase that dreamed-of post-and-beam house with soaring mountain views. We look out into Pleasant Valley, just over the line into New York State. A friend swears that this is the exact view that Grandma Moses painted over and over. The sole outbuilding is a small garden shed, but Tony is putting up a yurt for a private writing studio. At one end of the house where, I suppose, my separate office for seeing clients might have gone, is an outsized bathroom. The tub has huge floor-to-ceiling windows on two sides. Depending on time of day and season, one can bathe and look out at the birds at the feeder, fireflies, stars, or wild turkeys in full regalia. I work in a corner of the living room framed by heavy pine beams. I choose my clothes with luxurious indifference and wear soft shoes that make no echo.

Before medication my life's project was to understand my pain. I was ill and in my illness made the mistake of treating my symptoms as metaphors. I tried to ascribe meaning to them. And I understand the impulse behind that quest. Pain that is part of a coherent story is tolerable. Pain without meaning is unbearable.

But this proved a dangerous exercise. The pain had no meaning beyond the brute fact of it.

Sure there is a story to each of our lives. But it's not necessarily for our therapeutic perusal and re-perusal. For the psychotherapy patient is the ultimate unreliable narrator — a literary term to describe instances when the person relaying the story cannot wholly be trusted, as he is speaking through his or her limited perspective. A person's story is not stable; it alters with the telling and with the audience. When in therapy I described my childhood, it was cloaked in a Gothic pall. When I look at old photographs, I see me and my brother giggling conspiratorially and pushing bubbles at each other in the bath, closer to a G-rated family comedy. As with most of us, the reality is probably some mixture of the two.

Can a therapist tease out memories of emotional states from current emotional states? In attempting to do so in therapy are we uncovering truth or making fiction? I don't know. But one thing I do know: now that I am blessed with the capacity to do so I want to be in the story, not merely dissect it. I want a life that's more than the sum of therapy hours.

Of course, I have low days. I get as disturbed as anyone about world events and worry about the mess my son's generation stands to inherit. I get bored, frustrated, and extremely anxious about our bank account. It has taken time for Tony and me to find our way back to each other. Beyond that, I get colds and lots of stomachaches (an unpleasant effect of medication has been a pretty messed-up gastrointestinal tract.) And as the winters drag on (and on…), well, every Vermonter will recognize that mud season of the mind.

If a bad mood persists I am frightened to realize that my thoughts still run downhill. My medication gives me options, not direction. There are those who say antidepressants create a floor of mood that they never dip beneath. That is not the case with me. My emotional state is more like a floating ball that comfortably hovers a bit higher than it used to.

I have learned to befriend my brain. I read its responses, trying to tune in to what it's telling me (that perhaps I'm tired, over stimulated, need to check in with myself.) I make feeling good a priority so as to keep that floating ball aloft. If I start wallowing I've got to get myself out of it. In her book *A Life of One's Own*, British psychoanalyst Marion Milner (writing as Joanna Field) observed her own thoughts and feelings over a period of time and wrote about what she learned about emotional life. In a chapter entitled "The Coming and Going of Delight" she described how, when pensive or bored, she could moderate her mood by small shifts in self-awareness. She called these perceptual modulations "internal gestures of the mind." That's about as good a description as I can find for what I do. I believe that I have a responsibility to feel okay. Only when I feel okay can I access the energy, optimism, outrage, or wherewithal to do what I need to do. Only when I feel okay can I greet the world as it is.

Fiction writers talk about the importance of "earning the ending." Basically, what this means is that the events in a given work are plausible. Does the novel's denouement make sense or does it seem contrived? If the protagonist falls in love, will the reader believe he is capable of falling in love? Maybe I didn't "earn" the ending I got, and didn't get the ending I worked toward. So what? Literature isn't life. And there's nothing so bracing as an O'Henry twist in the plot.

Besides, this isn't even the ending.

So this is where I depart from Freud, the neo-Freudians, post-neo-Freudians, etc. But wait — old Sigmund did have plenty of worthwhile stuff to tell us. One bit of wisdom was that psychoanalysis could not promise freedom from sadness and care, rather that one went from neurotic misery to "ordinary unhappiness". Glad I got that misery out of the way. As for what's left — dealing with life as it is — I'm not sure that I would use the term "unhappiness". And after where I've been, I would call it extraordinary.

Acknowledgements

Many thanks are owed to friends and readers, including Dina Elenbogen, Martine Byer, Cathy Wetzel, Christina Engelsgaard, Lizzie Harris McCormick, Elizabeth Kaplan, Jim Shepard, Dan Hofstadter, Michael Anderson, Gabrielle Rynes, and Amy Anselmo. Gratitude beyond words is due to my family for loving and putting up with me when I'm sure it wasn't easy. I also particularly want to note Stephen Cole, MD, who changed if not saved my life and who has since passed away and is much missed.

About the Author

Judith D. Schwartz is a writer with work published in venues as varied as *The New York Times*, the *Christian Science Monitor*, *Time.com*, *Glamour*, and *Redbook*. She is the author of *The Mother Puzzle: A New Generation Reckons with Motherhood* and co-author of *Tell Me No Lies: How to Face the Truth and Build a Loving Marriage* and others. A graduate of Brown University and The Columbia University Graduate School of Journalism, she lives in Southern Vermont with her husband, writer Tony Eprile, and their son, Brendan.